TOUNSI in BLACK & WHITE

AN IMMERSIVE, BILINGUAL
PICTIONARY

WITH OVER 800 DUOTONE IMAGES
FOR MASTERING TUNISIAN DERJA

PAUL R. BEEMAN
KHALED ARRES

Ω Lancer Learning Communities

Written and illustrated by Paul R. Beeman.
Edited and Translated by Khaled Arres

Published by Lancer Learning Communities, LLC.

ISBN   978-1-958941-27-0 (Paperback)
        978-1-958941-28-7 (Hardcover)

1st Printing: October 2024

Lancer Learning Communities, LLC
learn@lancercommunities.com
www.lancercommunities.com

PREFACE

TOUNSI in BLACK and WHITE is a visual dictionary designed to immerse learners in Tunisian Derja. As the title suggests, it clearly and concisely presents Tounsi in "Black and White" using duotone images and Latin script.

Tunisian Arabic, often referred to as Derja, is a beautiful language with its own distinct characteristics. While it shares similarities with standard Arabic, it has evolved over time, integrating Latin, Turkish, Berber, Italian and French. A reflection of the unique cultural and historical heritage of Tunisia.

Featuring over 860 essential words and phrases, we believe this book will be invaluable for anyone integrating into Tunisian society. As a reference document, it is not a comprehensive curriculum. We recommend combining it with language lessons from a qualified teacher or school to fully grasp the nuances and structure of the language.

We chose to use Latin script for this book because it is familiar to those from English-speaking backgrounds. In considering the use of Arabic script, we found that Tunisian pronunciation often deviates from standard Arabic rules. Using Latin script allows us to accurately represent the sounds of Derja without forcing our intended audience to relearn phonetic symbols or Arabic writing.

The phonetic chart included in this book provides a guide to the pronunciation of the symbols used in this book. These same symbols are consistent with those found on street signs in Tunisia, making it easy to connect the written word with its spoken counterpart.

We love speaking Tounsi and hope that **TOUNSI in BLACK and WHITE** will be a valuable tool for anyone interested in learning this vibrant and expressive language. With dedication and practice, you too can master Derja and unlock the richness of Tunisian culture.

MarHabé bik fi Tounes,

Paul & Khaled

Phonetic Chart

Symbol	English Equivalent	French Equivalent	Arabic Symbol	Example
Vowels				
a	wall, car, saw	à, Paris, appeler	ا, ع	avril
Ä	Deep elongated "a" as in awe.	"à" de profondeur de la bouche	ع	sbÄ
e	elephant, end	blesser, tenir	ء	ekhel
é	cake, bait, bale	lait, saler, thé		éna
o	go, no, so	dos, eau, moto	و	Octobr
u	glue, new, two	tu, rue, mouton	و	bu
i	wing, sing, read	si, ni, lit	يْ	fil
w	wait, win, owe	oui, toillette	وْ	warqa
Consenants				
b	bike, beat, bat	bague, beau	ب	bÄid
d	do, duck, did	dire, doux	د	dabbuza

Symbol	English Equivalent	French Equivalent	Arabic Symbol	Example
d͟h	t͟his, t͟he, t͟hen	Touchez la pointe de la langue à l'arrière de vos dents et émettez un son tout en déplaçant la langue des dents.	ذ	dhaw
f	f͟un, f͟ar	f͟ille, f͟ort	ف	faqqus
g	g͟o, g͟et	g͟âteau, g͟omme		garaj
g͟h	Gutteral "r" sound. Raise the back of the tongue towards the back roof of the mouth (almost touching) and produce a vibration by passing air between the tongue and the roof of the moth.	r͟ue, r͟ouge	غ (ghayn)	ghadwa
h	h͟at, h͟it, h͟ope	Un court souffle léger.	ه	mehbul
H, H	(stronger or breathier "h")	Un court souffle fort.	ح	Halib
k	k͟ite, c͟at, blac͟k	c͟adeau, c͟lé	ك	kabbut

Symbol	English Equivalent	French Equivalent	Arabic Symbol	Example
kh	Place the tongue in the position of the "k" and aspirate like an "h". Like "loch" and "Bach"	Lève l'arrière de ta langue vers la partie molle du palais, souffle pour un son de gargouillement doux.	خ	khamsa
l	like, play, ball	lire, lent	ل	lah'ya
m	man, mud, time	main, manger	م	mÄeza
n	no, sin, pencil	neuf, non	ن	nHar
p	pen, pie, tap	père, pain	ب	Pakisténi
q	Uvular stop. Like "k" but the back of the tongue is positioned farther back.	quatre	ق	Qadesh
ɾ	A rolled "r", as in the Scottish accent "road" or "red".	Comme "rare" dans certain dialectes. Un "r" roulé.	ر	ras
s	sit, sand, miss	soupe, sac	س	sabÄ lef
S	A hard, exaggerated "S"	sacrifice, sombre	ص	ÄSfour
sh	sharp, mash, fish	chou, chat	ش	shA'ar
t	kit, sit, type	table, tout	ت	taHt

Symbol	English Equivalent	French Equivalent	Arabic Symbol	Example
T	Emphasized "t" as in Tap	N/A	ط	yfTor
th	thin, thank, thick	Touchez la front de la langue au dessus de vos dents et émettez un souffle en déplaçant la langue des dents.	ث	thmenin
v	van, vine, have	voiture, vin		valiz
y	yes, yellow	yeux, yaourt	ي	yabÄth
z	zoo, zip, has	zèbre, zéro	ز	zbib

Table of Contents
fahres

Nouns - Esemi

Verbs - afÄl

Descriptions - Šifet

Phrases - jumel

ESEMI
NOUNS

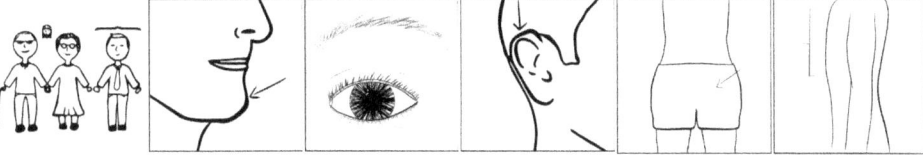

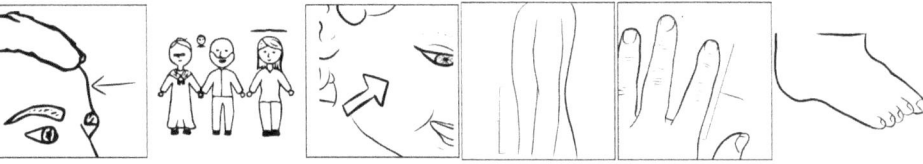

DHAMEERE
PRONOUNS

howa, hiya

he she

éna

I

huma

they

aĦna

we

enti

you

entuma

you all

NÉS
PEOPLE

tFol / tofla / bébé

baby

uled

boy

bnéya

girl

rajel

man

mRa

woman

sgha'ar

children

tbib

doctor

elHiméya l'medenéyya

fireman

ÄILLA
MEMBERS OF THE FAMILY

bu | baba

father

om | omi

mother

uled

son

bnéya

daughter

mra

wife

rajel

husband

elwldin

parents

kupl

couple

khuwét

siblings

khu kbir

big brother

okht kbira

big sister

khu sghir

little brother

ort sghira

little sister

jed

grandfather

jdda

grandmother

bent wldi | bent benti

granddaughter

wld wldi | wld benti

grandson

Hamé

in-laws

nsib

son in-law

kenna

daughter in-law

BDEN
PARTS OF THE BODY

yd

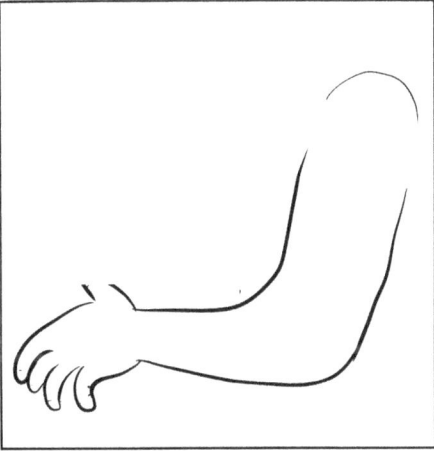

arm

dh'har

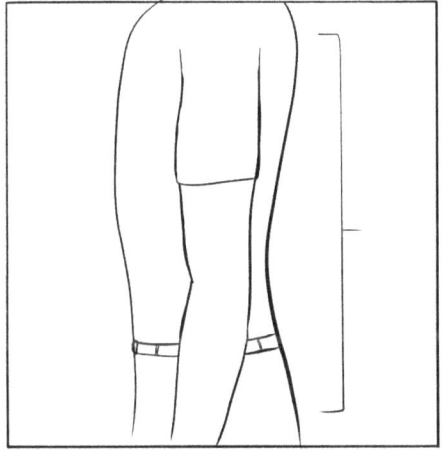

back

wora

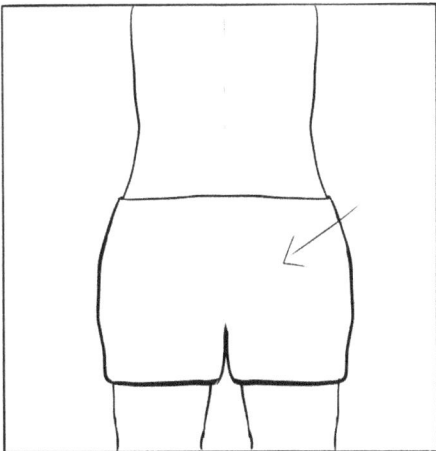

behind

kersh

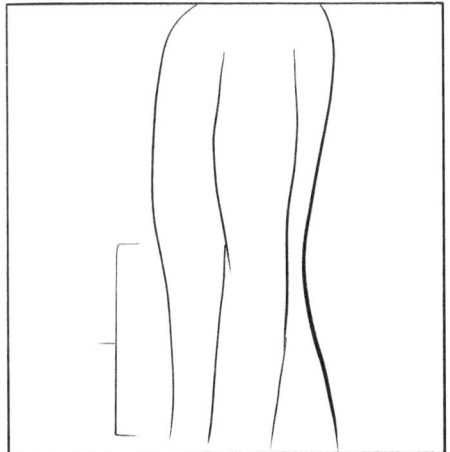

belly

khad

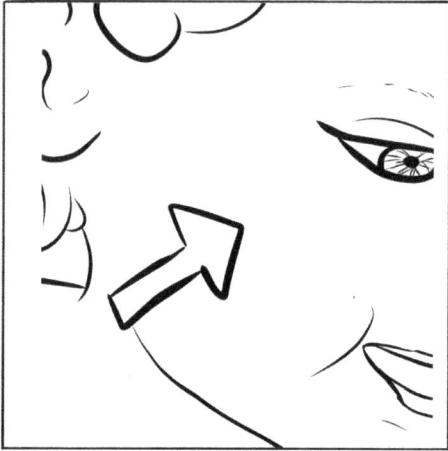

cheek

sder

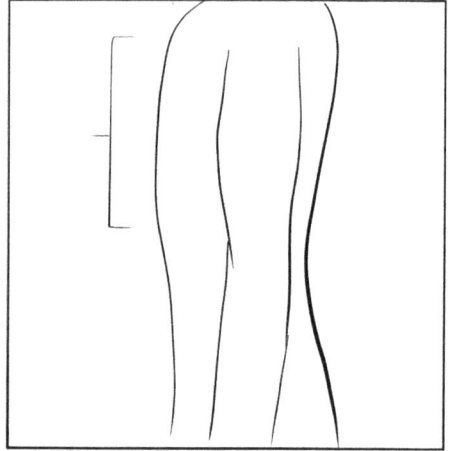

chest

dagnu'na

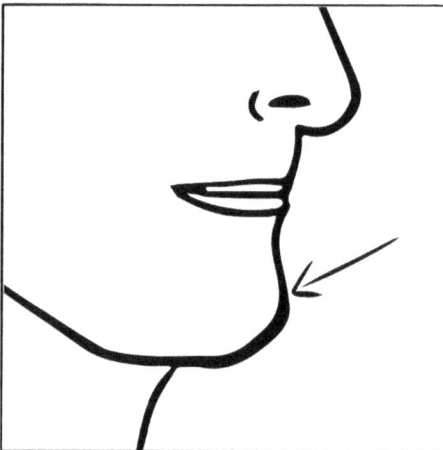

chin

odhen

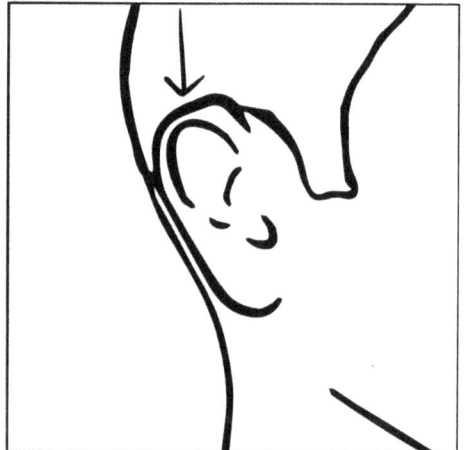

ear

marfaq

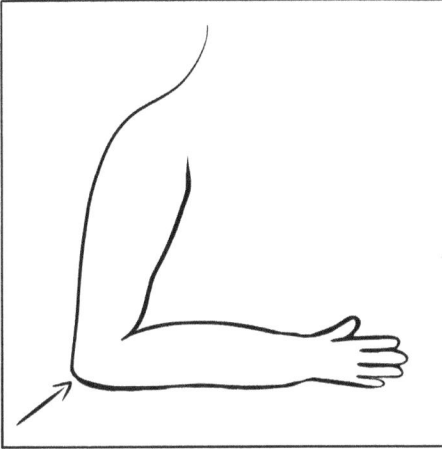

elbow

Äyn

eye

Ħajeb

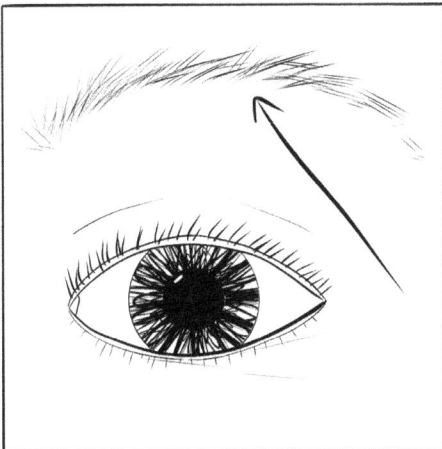

eyebrow

sbÄ

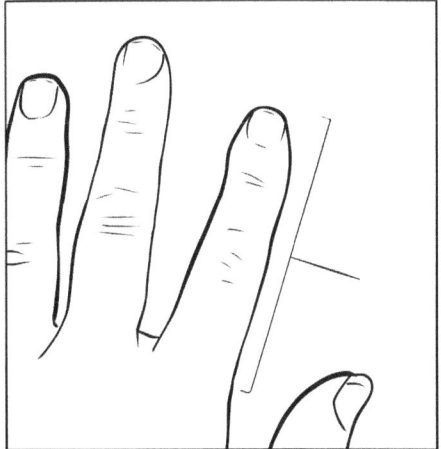

finger

Seq

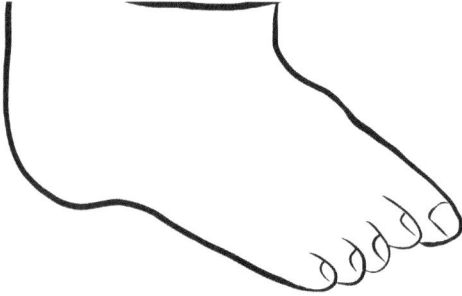

foot

jbin

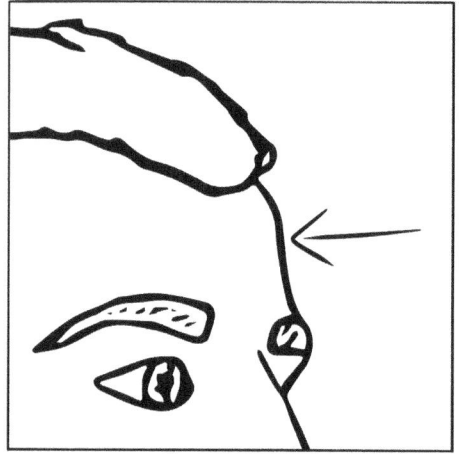

forehead

sh<u>Ä</u>'r

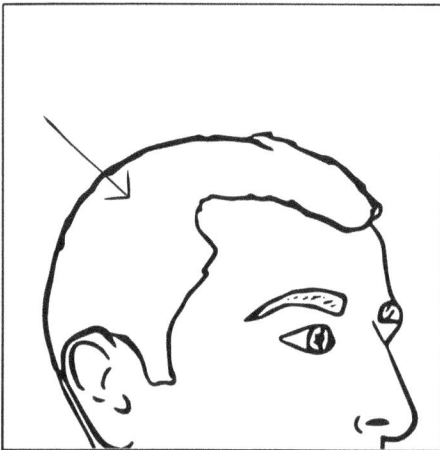

hair

yed

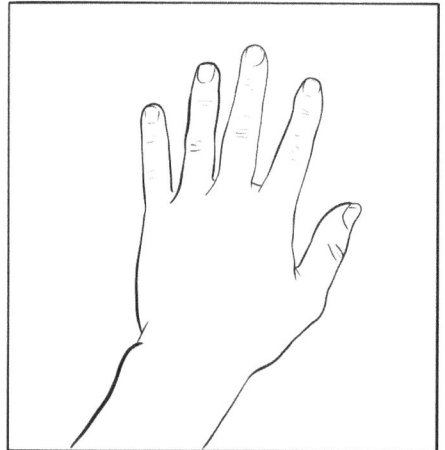

hand

PARTS OF THE BODY - NOUN - BDEN

ras

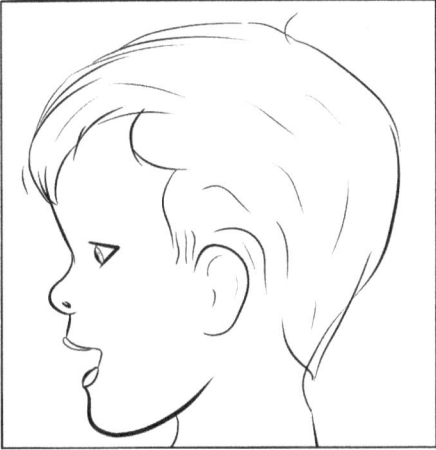

head

Hzém

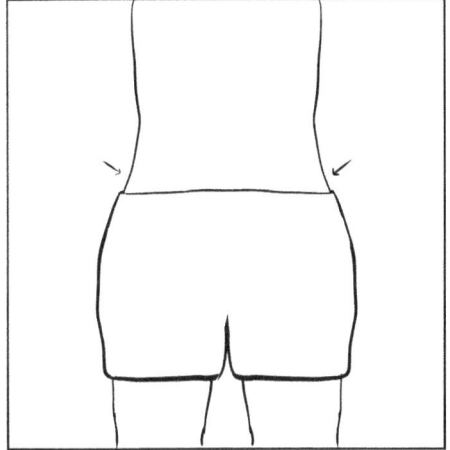

hips

jdeq

jaw

rokba

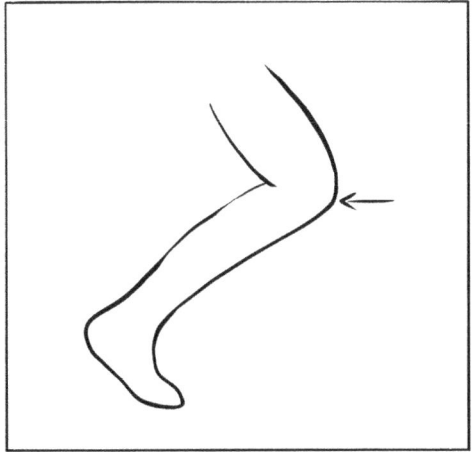

knee

Seq

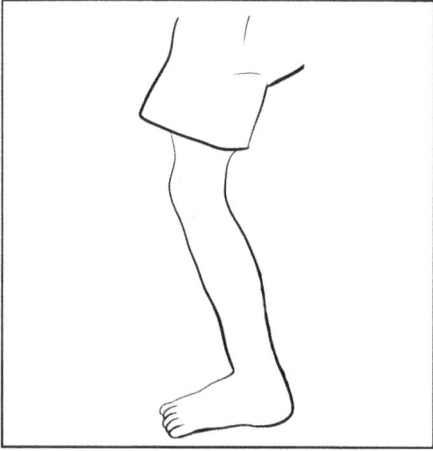

leg

fom

mouth

khashm

nose

ktf

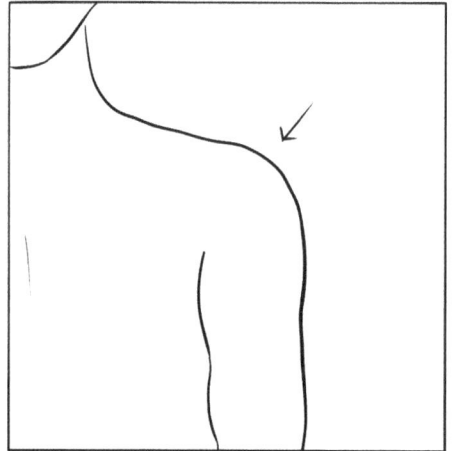

shoulder

garjuma

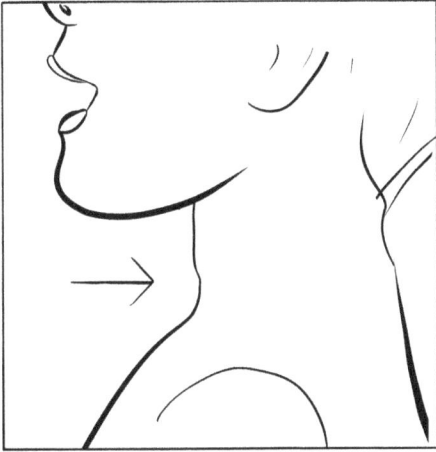

throat

swébÄ'a saqin

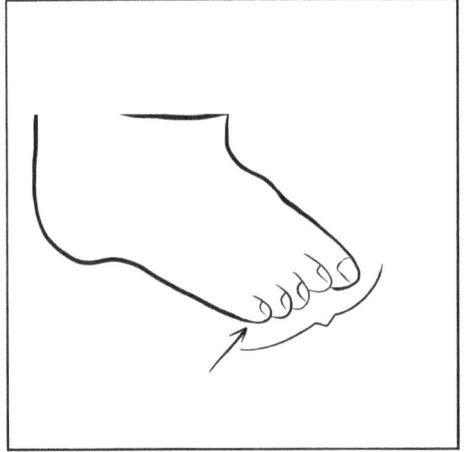

toes

laH'ya

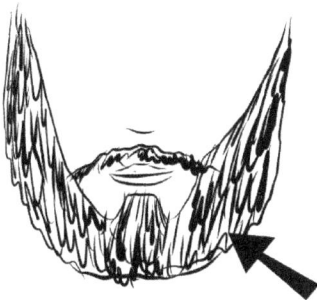

beard

shlégham

mustache

ḤAYUWANET
ANIMALS

ÄSfour

bird

qtousa

cat

bagra

cow

kelb

dog

Ħuta

fish

dhebbéna

fly

jrana

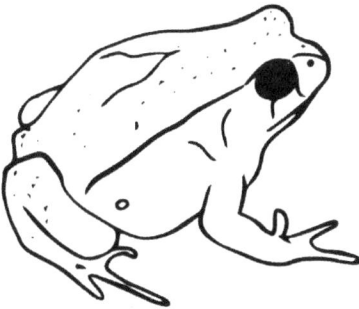

frog

ĦaSan

horse

far

mouse

ankabuta

spider

naHla

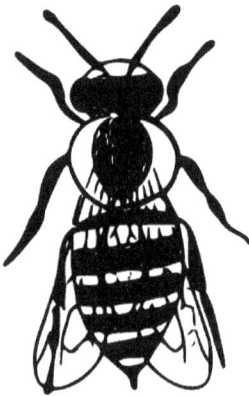

bee

jmel

camel

ANIMALS - NOUN - ĦAYUWANET

djéja

chicken

btta

duck

fil

elephant

mÄza

goat

wezza

goose

sid

lion

saHaléya

lizard

khnzir

pig

arneb

rabbit

Älloush

sheep

Ḥanesh

snake

nmr

tiger

BDEN ḤAYUWANET
ANIMAL PARTS

mongar

beak

dhfar

claw

riysh

feather

wbar

fur

Ḥawéfr

hooves

garn

horn

kméma

muzzle

qawqÄ

shell

dhil | baÄbous   # khartum

tail

trunk

jnéH   # jnéH

wing

wing

ESHKEL
SHAPES

dura

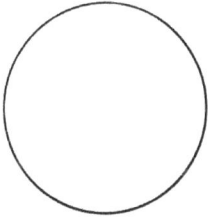

circle

mustatil

rectangle

kura

sphere

murabbÄ

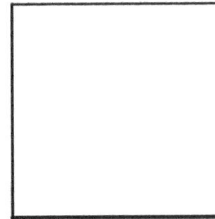

square

mutheleth

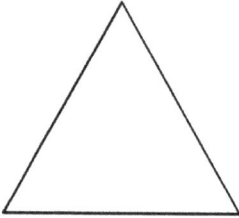

triangle

kurnu

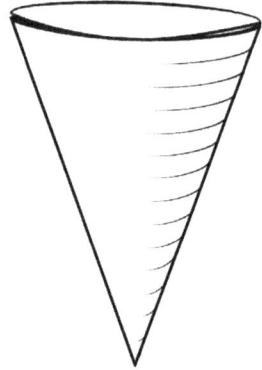

cone

moukaÄb

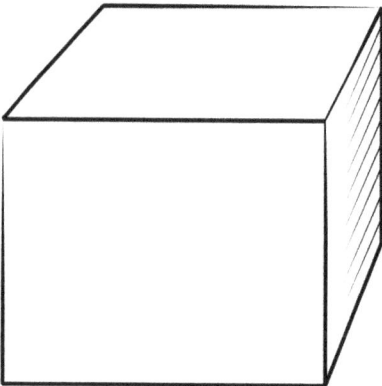

cube

si'lendr

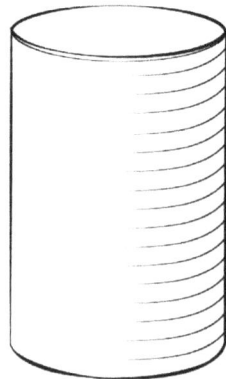

cylinder

khatt

khumési

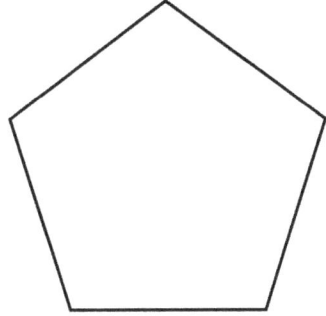

line

pentagon

harem

nejma

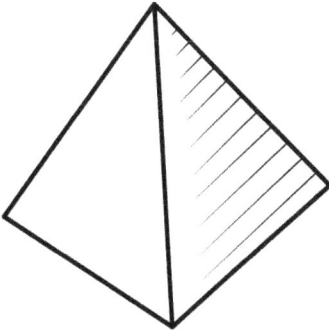

pyramid

star

TRANSPORTASION
VEHICLES

fluka

boat

battu

ship

ambilans

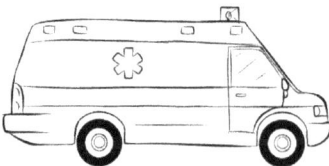

ambulance

kar

bus

karhaba

car

transportur

delivery truck

mutor

motorcycle

kamyun

pickup truck

vspa

scooter

Trino

train

bysklet

bicycle

hilikoptr

helicopter

VEHICLES - NOUN - TRANSPORTASION

ḤAWÉJ
CLOTHING

kasqet

baseball hat

sebta

belt

bluzah

blouse

bot

boot

<u>shesh</u>éya

cap

kabbut

coat

ruba

dress

suréya

dress shirt

sabat

dress shoe

gwandouwet

gloves

Talon

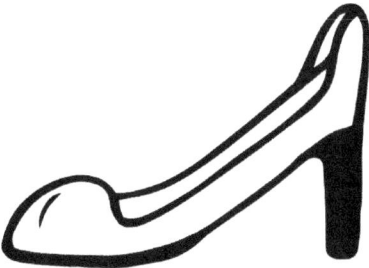

high heels

kapu<u>sh</u>

hoodie

vista

jacket

jiin

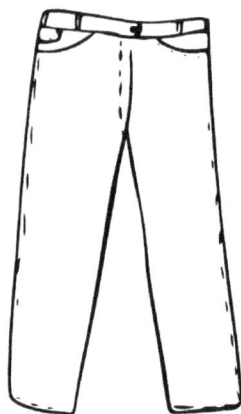

jeans

mini-jup

mini skirt

seruwel

pants

kap du ban

robe

sandel

sandal

sandel

sandals

ka<u>sh</u> kol

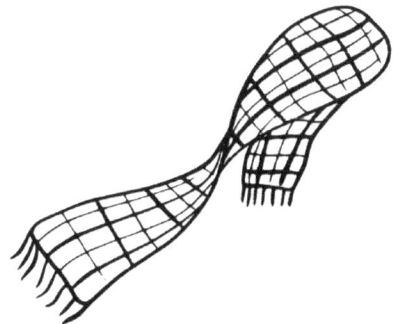

scarf

shmiz

shirt

short

shorts

jbah

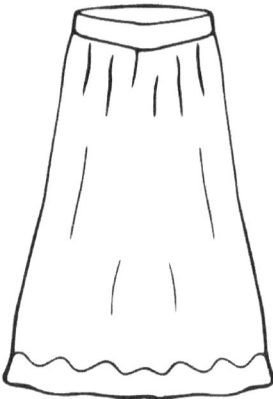

skirt

sbedriy

sneaker

klaset

socks

kostum

sports coat

marioul <u>khshin</u>

sweater

marioul

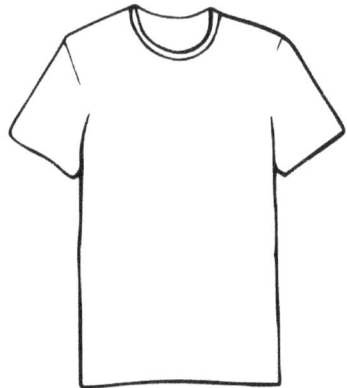

t-shirt

marioul <u>khl</u>Ä'a

tank top

kravat

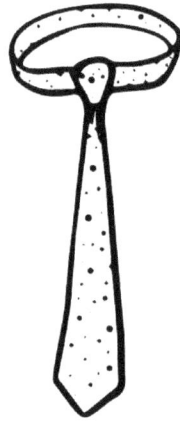

tie

marioul

tunic

slip

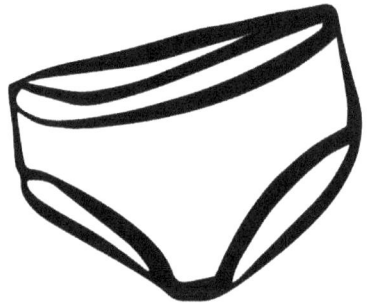

underwear

jilé

vest

jiyliyya

vest

tarbusha

winter hat

Ħwé'yj

clothes

FI WSET MEDINA
AROUND TOWN

dar

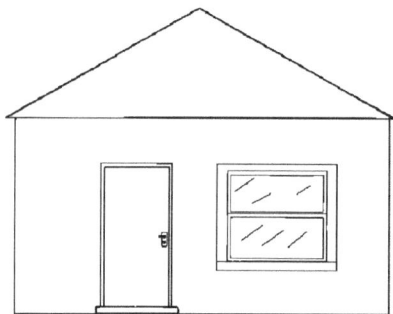

house

zriba

barn

sénia

field

méda

sidewalk

matar

airport

balas

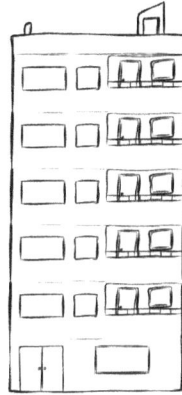

apartment building

kousha

bakery

banka

bank

bar

bar

Ḥajém

barbershop

maḤattat kiran

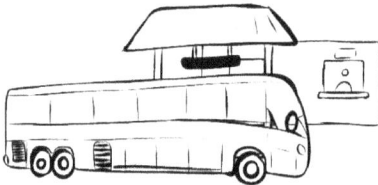

bus station

jza'ar

butcher

knisiyya

church

Hanut Ħwéj

clothing store

qahwa | kafé

coffee shop

tbib snin

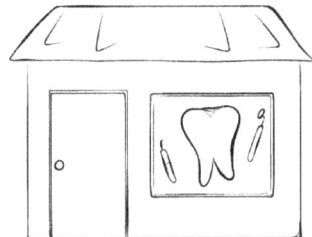

dentist

magazan

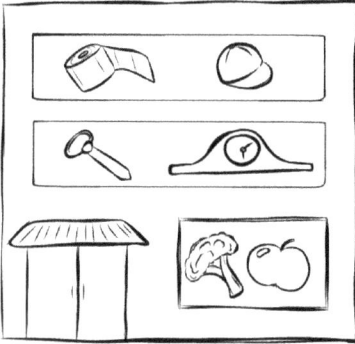

department store

kabin tbib

doctor's office

nwa'wari

florist

muftaraq

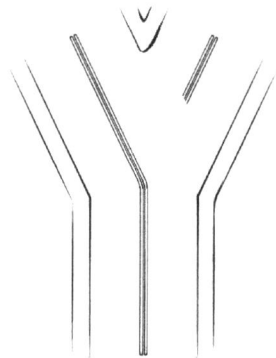

fork in the road

khdhar

fruit stand

magazen d'mobl

furniture store

kiosk

gas station

Ḥajema

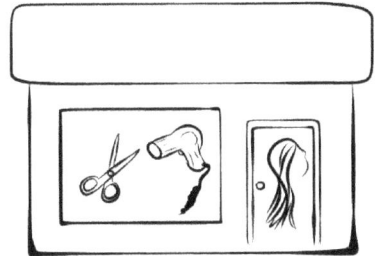

hair salon

kenqi'ouri

hardware store

sbitar

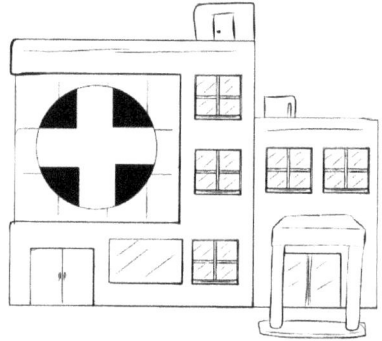

hospital

entirseksion

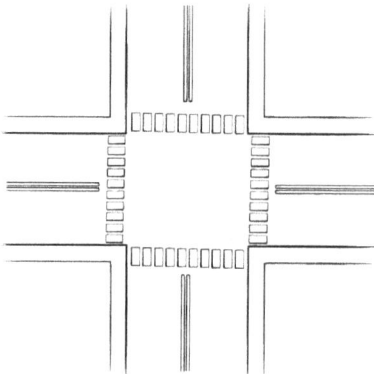

intersection

mektba

library

suq

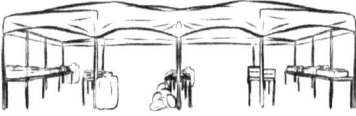

market

jémÄ

mosque

Hanout

newspaper stand

montazah

park

farmasi

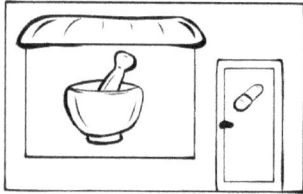

pharmacy

busta

post office

risto

restaurant

ron-pwa

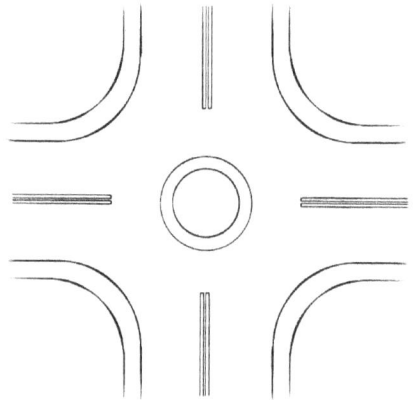

round point

madersa

school

mÄbed

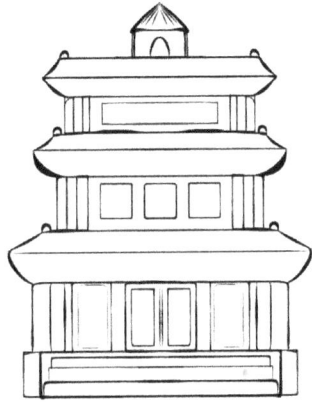

temple

borj

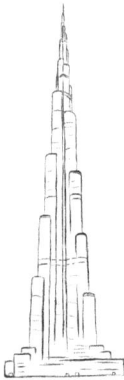

tower

butik ella'ab

toy store

maHatta trino

byuro

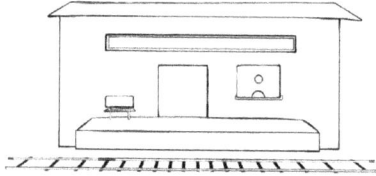

train station

office

FI DAR
AT HOME

farsh

bed

futey

chair

korsi

chair

divan

couch

kumidino

dresser

taoula

table

radiator

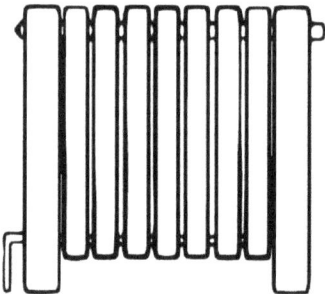

heater

gaz

stove

shobek

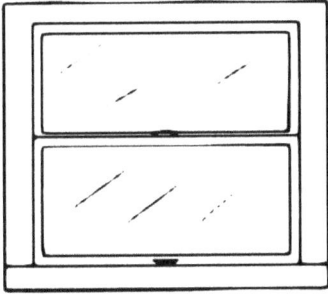

window

mréya

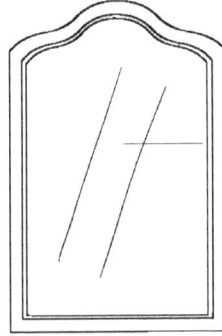

mirror

lavabouw

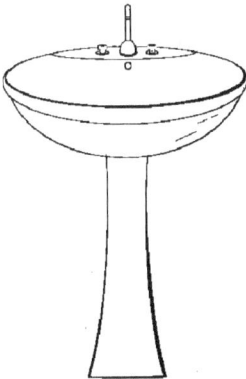

sink

twalet

toilet

jenina

garden

athéth

furniture

banu

bathroom

bit enum

bedroom

bit ftour

dining room

kulwar

hallway

kujina

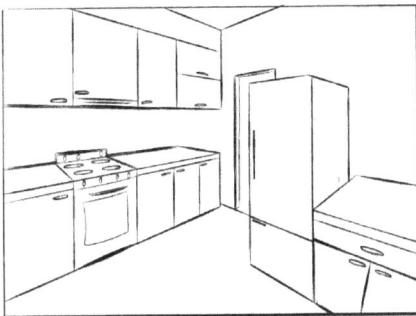

kitchen

salla

living room

MÉKLA
FOOD

lu'uz

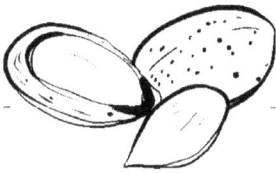

almond

tuféH

apple

bnan

banana

Hbaq

basil

bitarav

beet

<u>khubz</u>

bread

brokli

broccoli

krumb

cabbage

gatu

cake

Halwa

candy

sfinne'rya

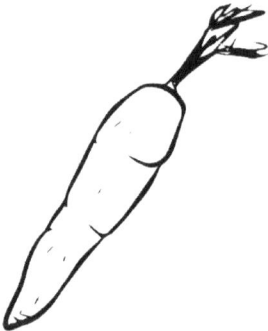

carrot

bruklu

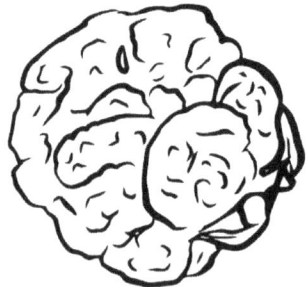

cauliflower

Ḥab mlu'k

cherry

kosbr

cilantro

beshqutu

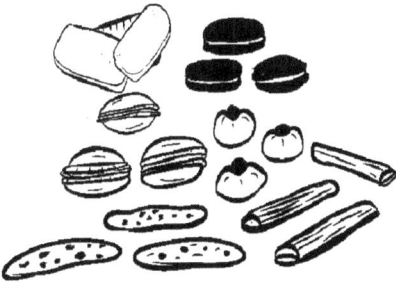

cookies

qTa'niyya

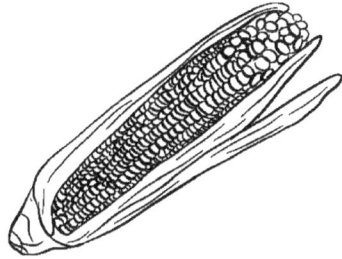

corn

faqqus

cucumber

Ädhma

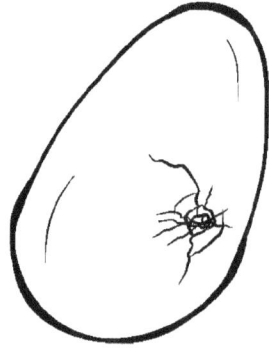

egg

bitenjel

eggplant

farina

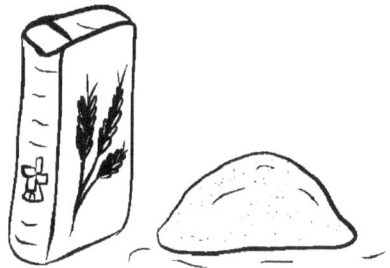

flour

thum

garlic

Äneb

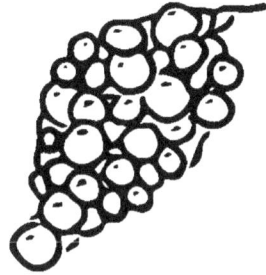

grapes

bsal ak<u>hd</u>hr

green onion

qares

lemon

slata

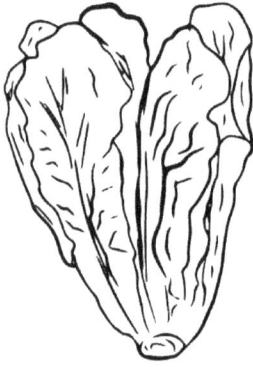

lettuce

ménga

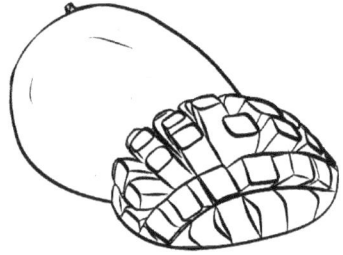

mango

elHam

meat

nanéÄ

mint

shampinion

mushrooms

zuza

nut

bsal

onion

bour'gdén

orange

mÄ'adnus

parsley

jelbéna

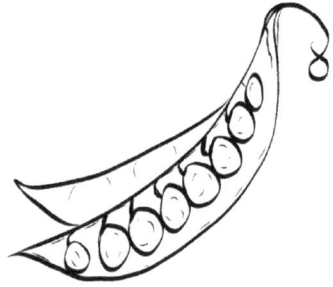

pea

kakawia

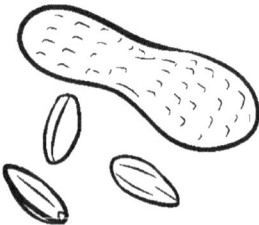

peanut

anzas

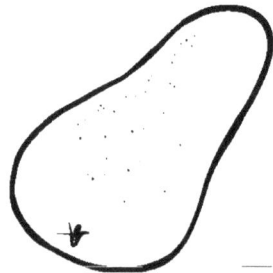

pear

felfel a<u>kh</u>el

pepper

felfel

pepper

ananas

pineapple

batata

potato

qrÄ

pumpkin

fjel

radishes

zbiyb

raisins

ruzz

rice

mlaH

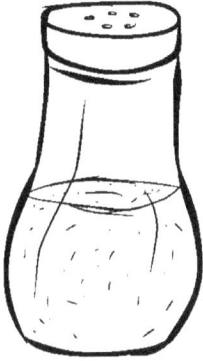

salt

frez

strawberry

sukkar

sugar

tamatam

tomato

dellé'Ä

watermelon

qraÄ akh<u>d</u>hr

zucchini

karbunatu

baking soda

g<u>h</u>alla

fruit

khudhra

vegetables

glass

ice cream

MÄOUN TANDHIF
CLEANING TOOLS

shi'ta

brush

zbla

trash

bala

dust pan

jabéda

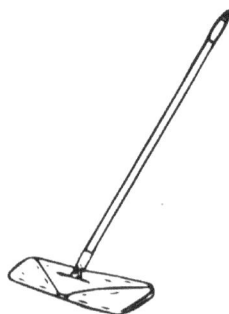

mop

aspirateur

makinet sabon

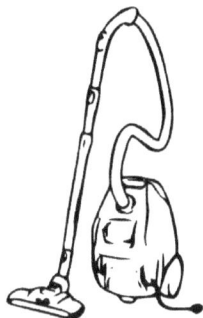

vacuum

washing machine

MASHRUBET
DRINKS

bier

beer

qahwa

coffee

gazuze

soda

té

tea

Äsir

juice

Hlib

milk

mé

water

ven

wine

MÄOUN KUJINA
FOOD UTENSILS

fargitta

fork

kés

glass

Sekkina

knife

saĦfa kbira

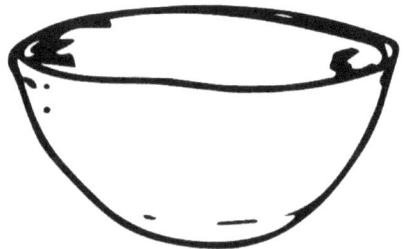

large bowl

saḤn kbir

large plate

Ḥaléb

mug

saḤfa sghira

small bowl

saḤn sghir

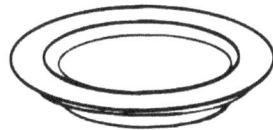

small plate

magharfa

spoon

kés té

teacup

barréd

teapot

kup

wineglass

qasasa

cutting board

maÄoun

dishes

baréd

kettle

ghta'a

lid

mé'Äoun

dishes

qaléya

pan

qomsan

pitcher

tanjra

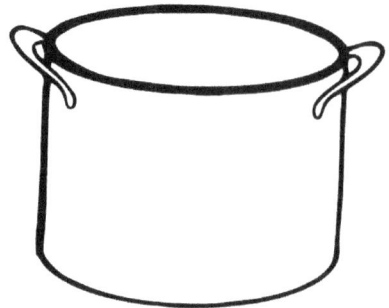

pot

qalaya

skillet

dabbu'za

bottle

mandila

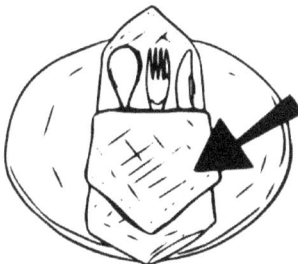

napkin

MÄOUN SANNÄ
TOOLS

fes

axe

vis

bolt

mtarqa

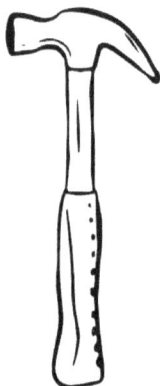

hammer

musmar

nail

boluna

nut

biynsa

plier wrench

pans

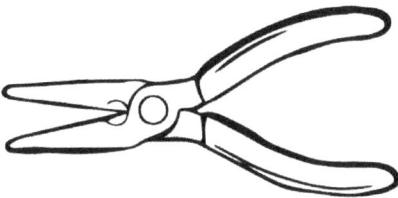

pliers

mon<u>sh</u>ar

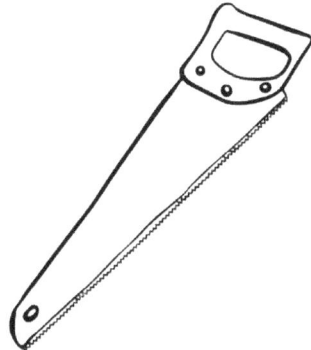

saw

viysa

screw

tournévis

screwdriver

tell

wire

mufté

wrench

ḤAJET
THINGS

ktéb

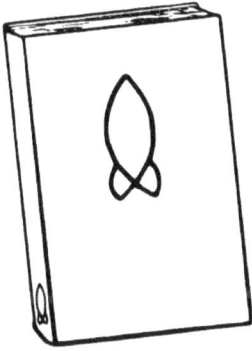

book

warqa

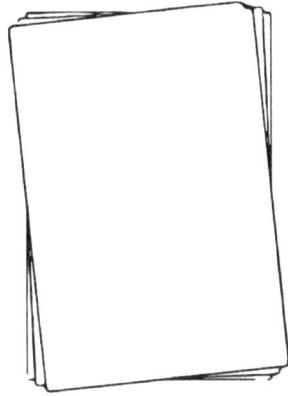

paper

stylo

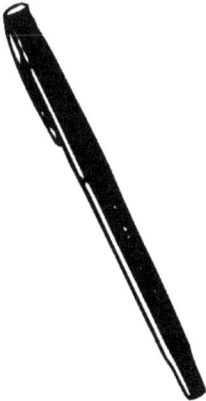

pen

klemersas

pencil

portable

phone

m<u>kh</u>ada

pillow

sabbura

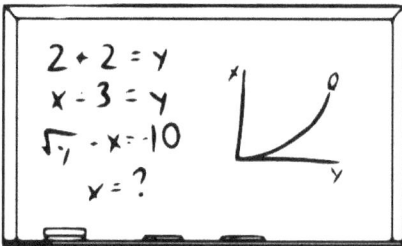

$$2 + 2 = y$$
$$x - 3 = y$$
$$\sqrt{-7} - x = -10$$
$$y = ?$$

board

mungéla

clock

mÄ'aleq

coat hanger

<u>dh</u>aw

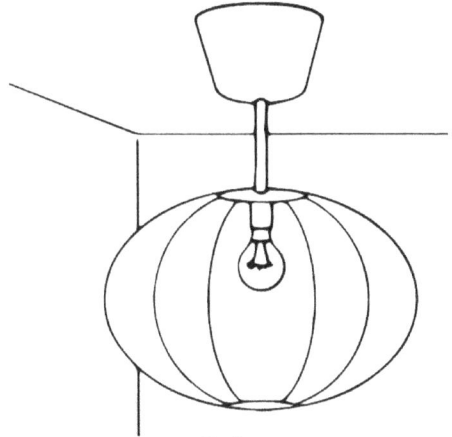

light

taswiyra

picture

Äoud uqid

match

mré'et

glasses

lsseq

glue

mqass

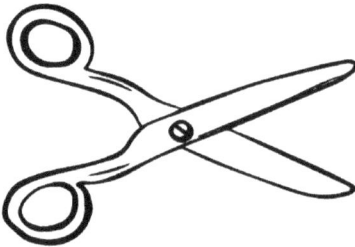

scissors

<u>kh</u>it

string

skotsh

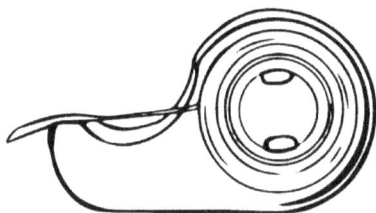

tape

knestru

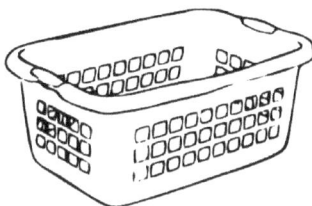

basket

farrashiyya

blanket

shaqshaqa

rattle

napp

table cloth

luwÄab

toys

sa<u>sh</u>é

bag

sak

purse

valiz

suitcase

s'Ħaba

umbrella

ŤABIÄA
NATURAL ELEMENTS

nawar

flower

s̲h̲ejara

tree

qaws quzah

rainbow

al-Älam

the world

shatt

beach

nepta

bush

s'Hab

cloud

saHara

desert

ghaba

forest

jbel

mountain

hinshiyr

orchard

bHar

sea

smé

sky

du<u>kh</u>an

smoke

<u>sh</u>ams

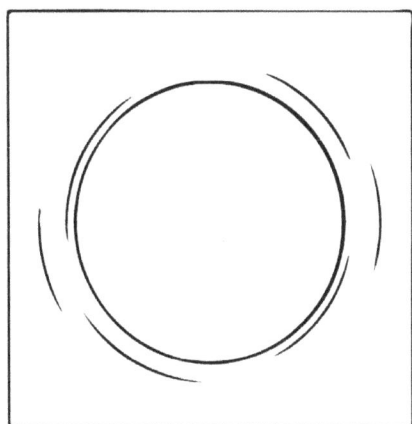

sun

wéd

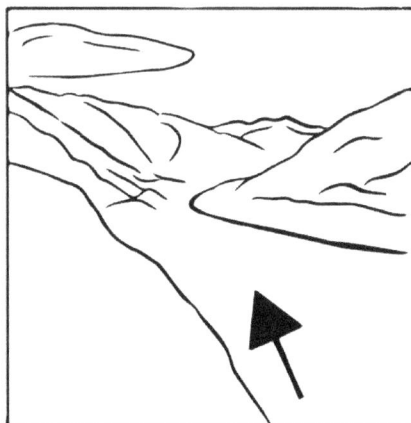

valley

muj

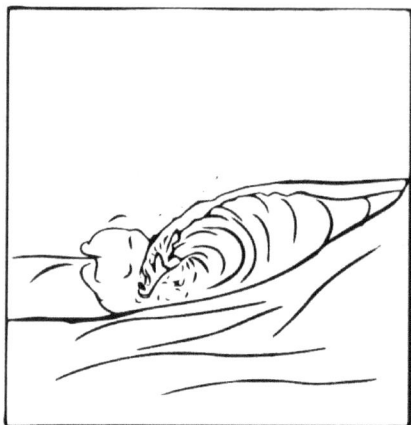

wave

NDHAFA
HYGEINE

khallas

comb

moushwar

handkerchief

lesqa | faSma

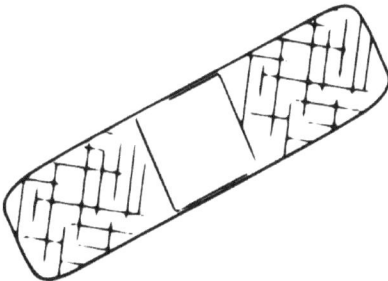

band aid

varniz

fingernail polish

shitet shÄar

hair brush

dwyé

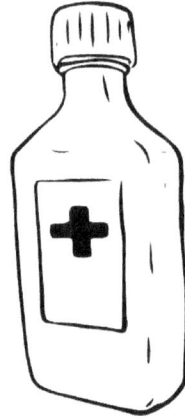

medicine

kup angl

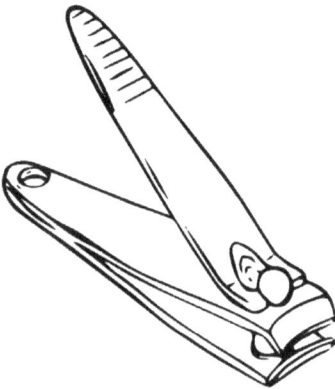

nail clippers

kunulya

perfume

Harab<u>sh</u>

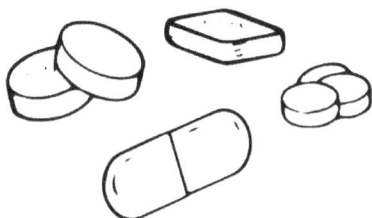

pills

makinet Ḥajema

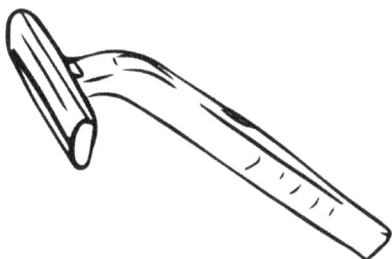

razor

sabun

soap

<u>sh</u>itet snin

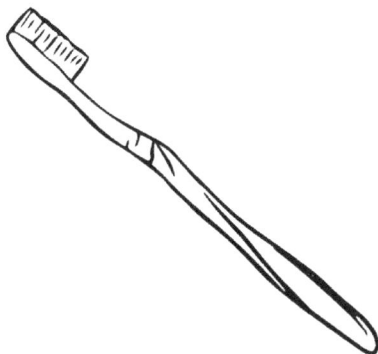

tooth brush

dentefris

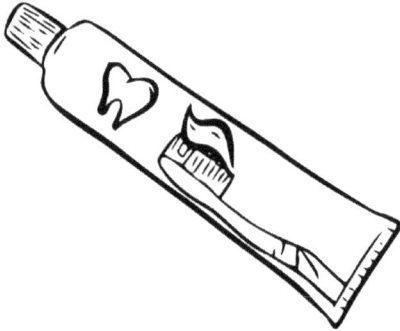

toothpaste

mnshfah

towel

ÄLEM
THE WORLD

kharita

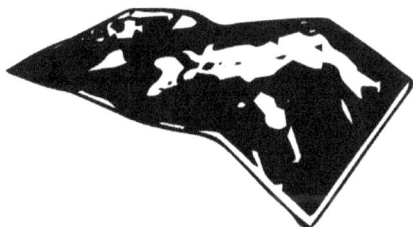

a map

l'afrik

africa

ésia

asia

ostraliya

australia

l'erop

europe

kura l'ar<u>dh</u>éya

globe

amrikia <u>sh</u>amaliyya

north america

amrikia al-janubiyya

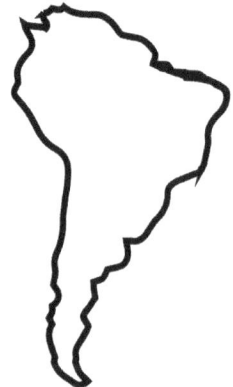

south america

FUŠUL
THE SEASONS

<u>kh</u>arif

fall

erbiÄ

spring

sif

summer

<u>sh</u>té

winter

sharq

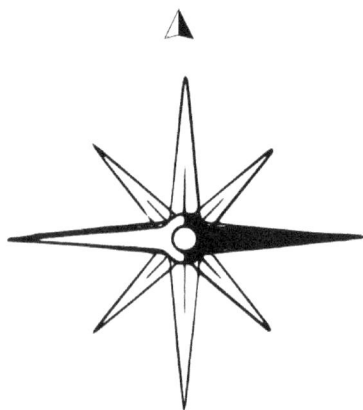

east

shemel

north

janub

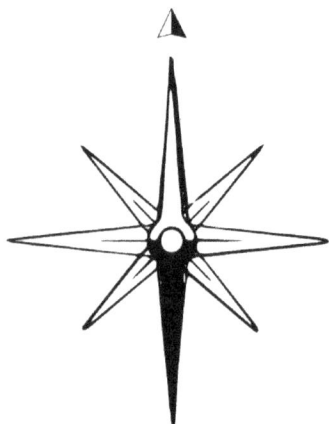

south

gharb

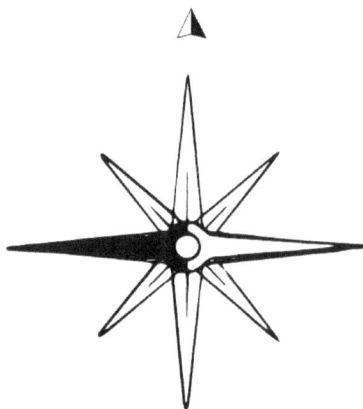

west

YAWMIYA
CALENDAR

nĦar | yom

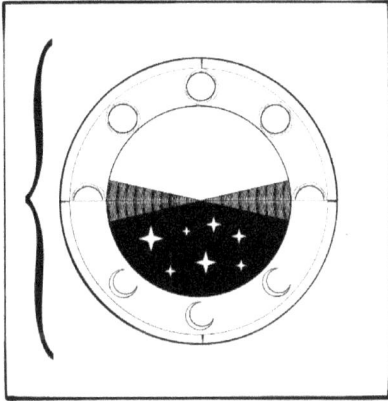

a day

jmÄ'a

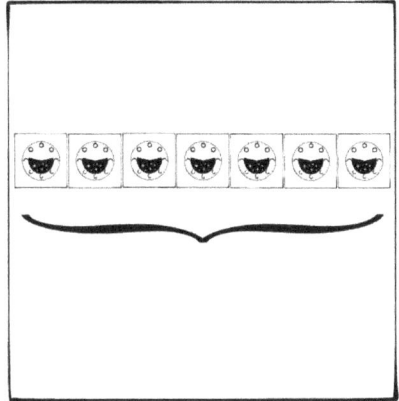

a week

sh'har

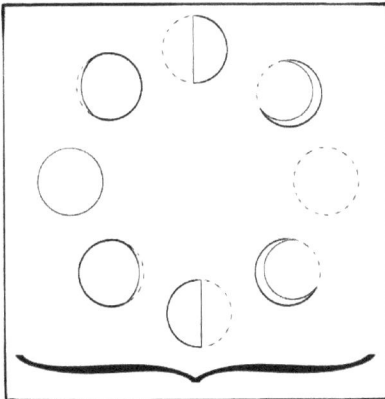

a month

Äm

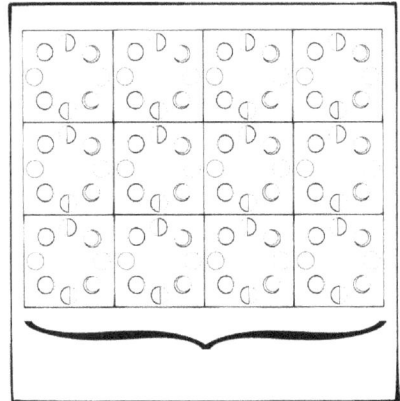

a year

nhar laHad

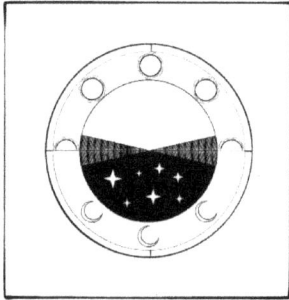

1

sunday

nhar ithnin

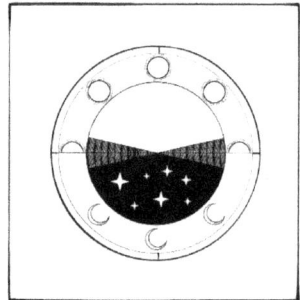

2

monday

nhar tlétha

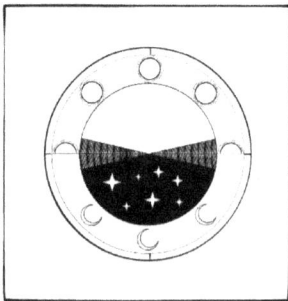

3

tuesday

nhar l'rbÄ

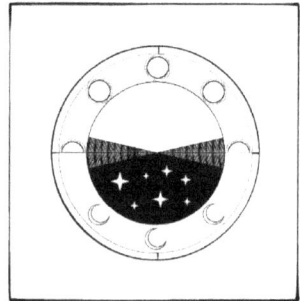

4

wednesday

nhar el-<u>kh</u>amis

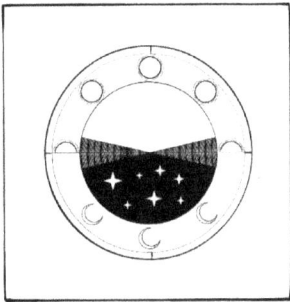

5

thursday

nhar el-jmÄ

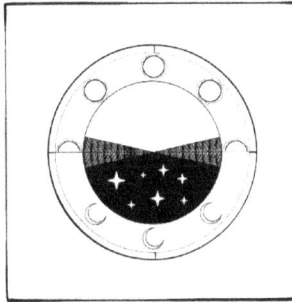

6

friday

nhar el-sbet

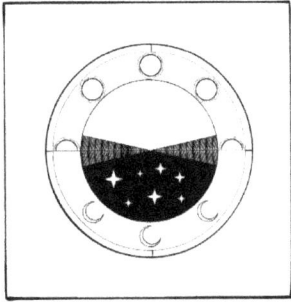

7

saturday

Janvi

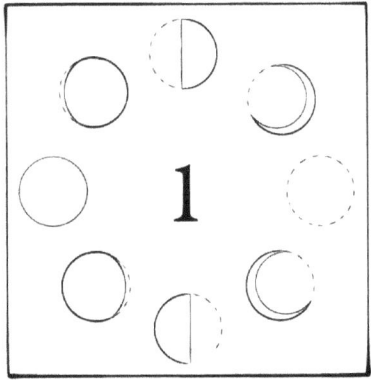

1

january

Fivri'

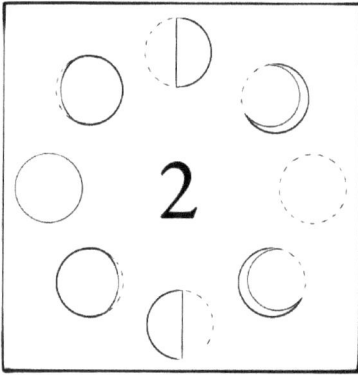

february

Mars

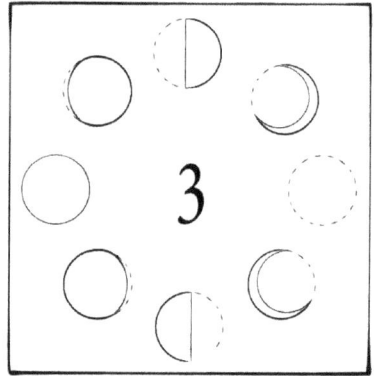

march

Avril

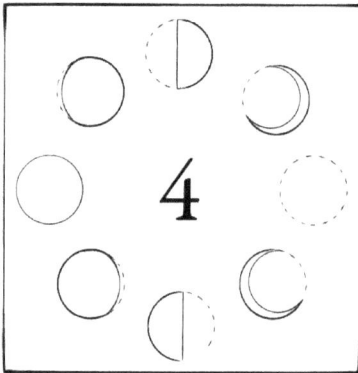

april

Mai

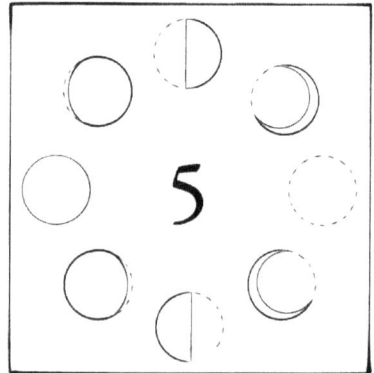

may

CALENDAR - NOUN - YAWMIYA

Juan

june

Juillia

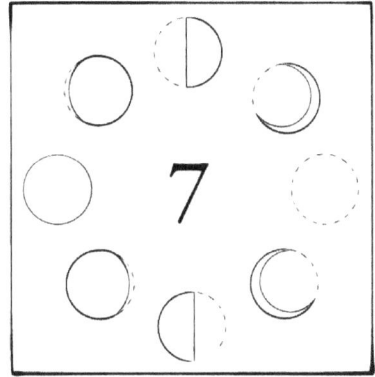

july

Out

august

Septembr

september

Oktobr

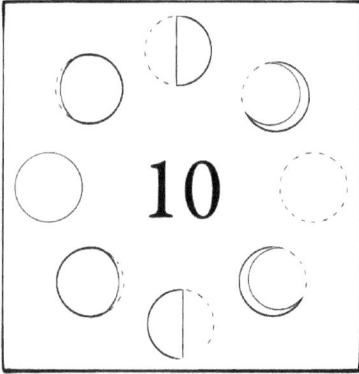

october

Novmbr

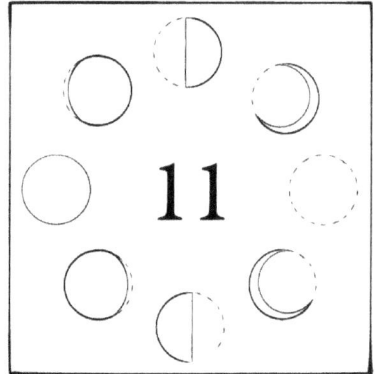

november

Desembr

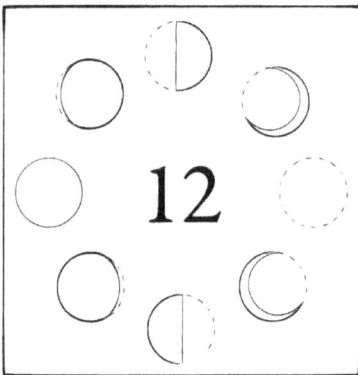

december

FLUS
MONEY

millim | frénk

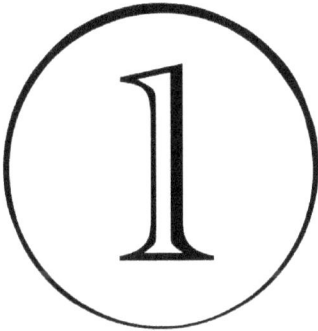

one cent

khamsa frénk

five cents

miet frénk

a hundred thousandths

alf frénk | dinar

a thousand thousandths

Äshara frénk

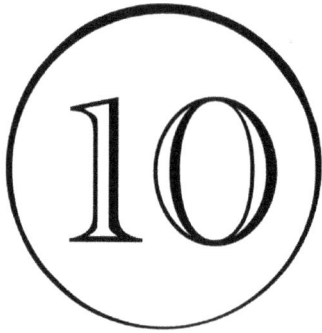

ten cents

khamsin frénk

fifty cents

khamsa miyé

five hundred thousandths

dinar

a dollar

MONEY - NOUN - FLUS

khamsa lef

Äshara lef

five dollars

ten dollars

khamsin elf

miét dinar

fifty dollars

a hundred dollars

khamsa miét elf

million

500

1000

five hundred dollars

a thousand dollars

khamsa mléyen

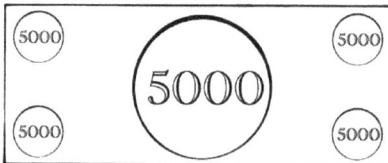

5000

five thousand dollars

MONEY - NOUN - FLUS

BENII
STRUCTURE

sqaf

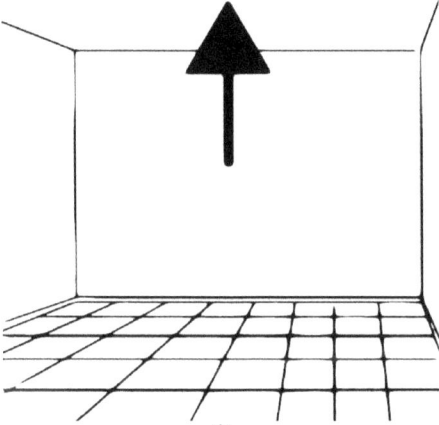

ceiling

kwa

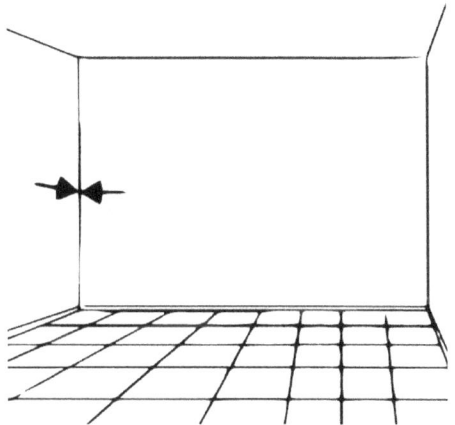

corner

béb

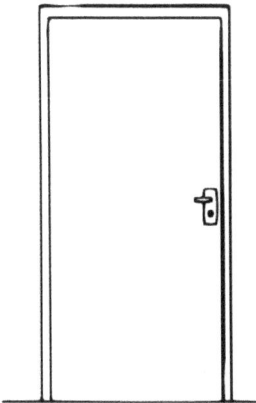

door

qÄ'a

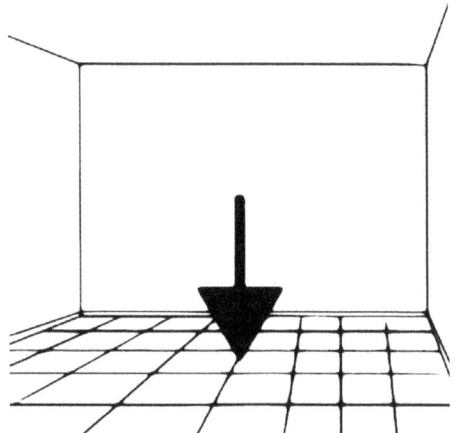

floor

Hit

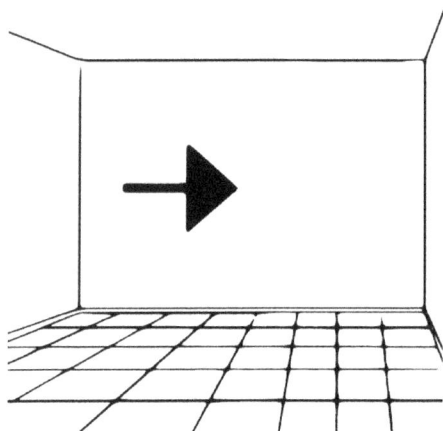

wall

suur

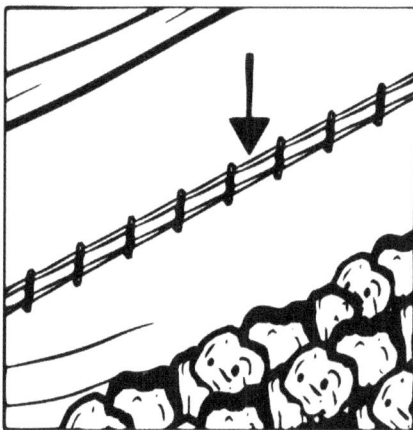

fence

garaj

garage

sTaH

roof

Hit

wall

sanba

statue

drouwj

staircase

nhar

lil

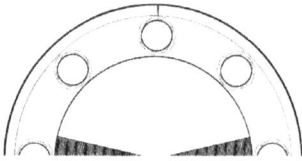

day

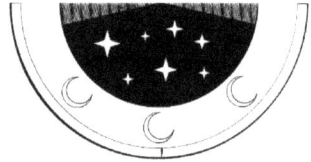

night

fejr

sbeH

dawn

morning

nos nhar

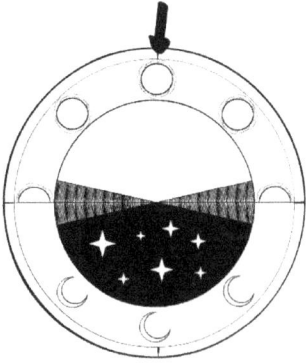

noon

qayla

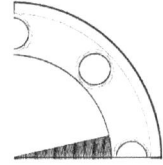

afternoon

lÄasheyya

evening

nos el-lil

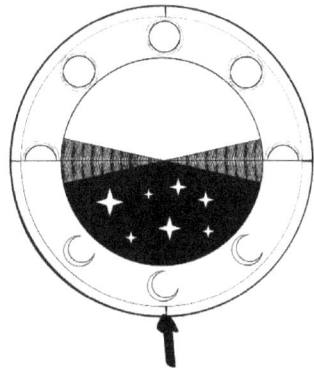

midnight

shuruq el-shemes

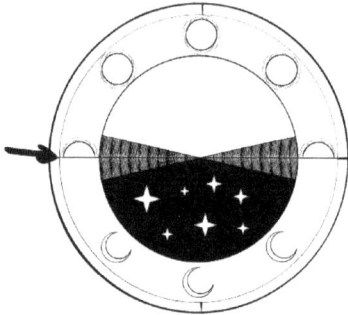

sunrise

ghurub el-shemes

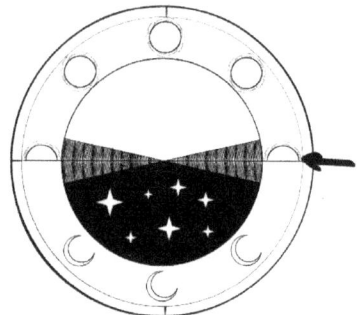

sunset

madhi sé'Ä

one o'clock

madhi sé'Ätin

two o'clock

TIME - NOUN - WAQT

madhi tlétha

three o'clock

l'arbÄ

four o'clock

l'khamsa

five o'clock

setta

six o'clock

Sa'abÄ

seven o'clock

thmenya

eight o'clock

tss'Ä

nine o'clock

madhi sé'Ätin ghir bÄ

one forty-five

l'Äsharah

ten o'clock

laḤde'sh

eleven o'clock

nos nhar | nos nlil

twelve o'clock

madhi sé'Ä u drej

one o'five

madhi sé'Ä u darjin

one ten

madhi sé'Ä u rbÄ

one fifteen

madhi sé'Ä u arbÄ

one twenty

madhi sé'Ä u nos

one thirty

TIME - NOUN - WAQT

l'yum

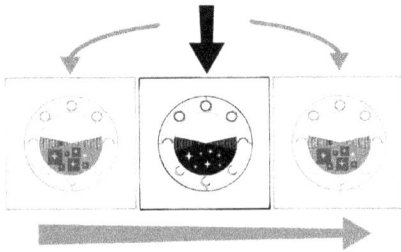

today

elberraⱧ

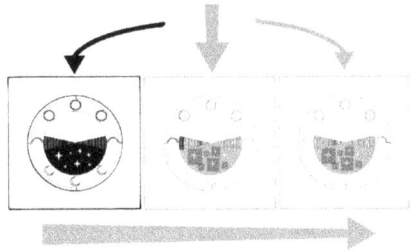

yesterday

g̲hdwa

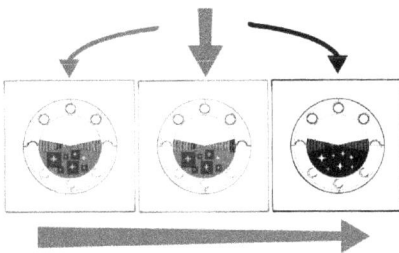

tomorrow

AFÄL

VERBS

YTHAREK
MOVEMENT

yji

to come

ym<u>sh</u>i

to go

ynegez

to jump

yorqod

to lie down

yjiri

to run

yqoÄd

to sit

yqum

to stand

ym<u>sh</u>i

to walk

MOVEMENT - VERB - YTHAREK

ytleffet

to turn around

ymil

to lean

yetalÄ

to climb

yaĦbu

to crawl

ysuq

to drive

ytir

to fly

ynegez fuq

to jump over

yerkb

to ride

MOVEMENT - VERB - YTHAREK

yerkb biskelt

to ride a bike

yerkb ĦaSan

to ride a horse

yÄom

to swim

ytlÄ

to walk up

HIWAR
COMMUNICATION

yÄti

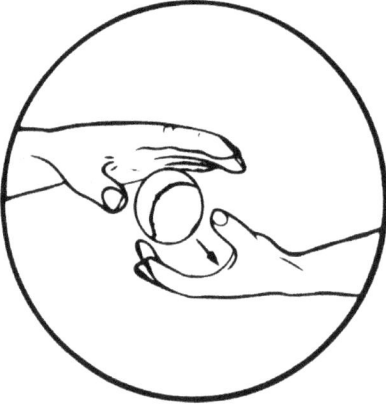

to give

ywari

to point

ywari

to show

ybki'i

to cry

yÄti

to give

ykteb

to write

y<u>kh</u>amem

to think

yi<u>sh</u>eri

to buy

ybi'Ä

to sell

ykelem

to call

yé<u>kh</u>u

to receive

yabÄ<u>th</u>

to send

ykashbr

to frown

yÄnaq

to hug

ybus

to kiss

ykhadhkhadh

to shake

yghani

to sing

ytbessam

to smile

yaHki

to talk

yghmez

to wink

MÉKLA
FOOD ACTIONS

ykos

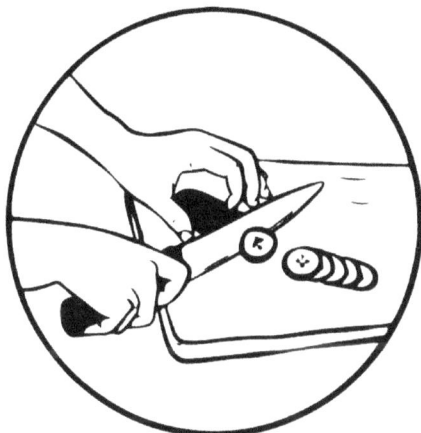

to chop

ytayeb

to cook

yshurb

to drink

yékal

to eat

yaghsel

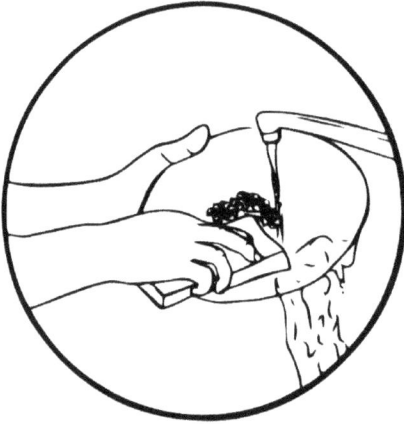

to wash

yÄdh | ygdem

to bite

yomghth

to chew

yblÄ

to swallow

ymlaH

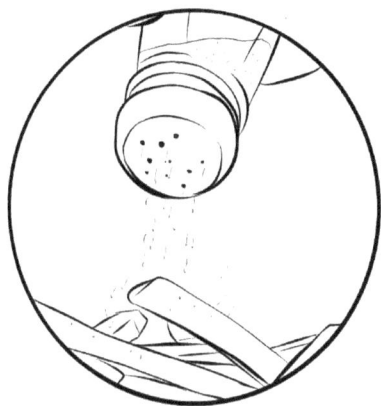

to salt

ŠAHA

HEALTH

yorqod

to sleep

yfiq men num

to wake up

yrtteH

to rest

yomkhat

to blow a nose

ykoH

to cough

yzafr

to exhale

ytnefes

to inhale

yÄ'ates

to sneeze

yjbd

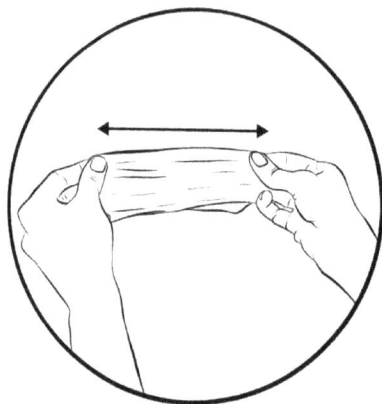

to stretch

yrod

to throw up

yTt͟héoub

to yawn

ÄMEL

INTERACTION

yoqaf

to stop

y<u>sh</u>uf

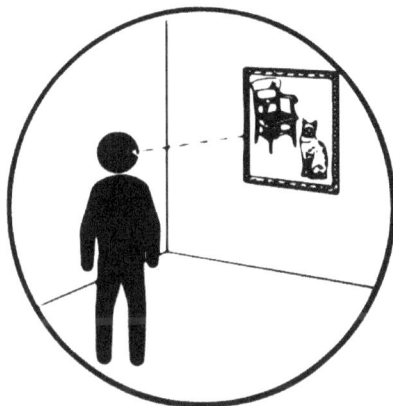

to look

yaqra

to read

yoqtl

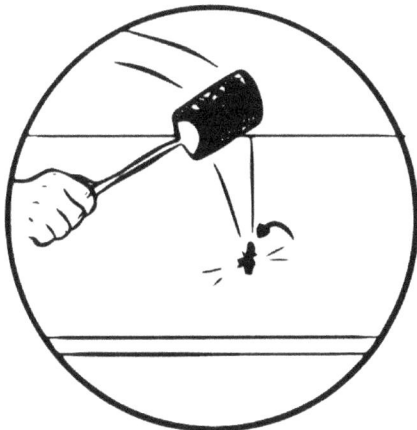

to kill

ylÄ'ab

to play

ykhdem

to work

ySali

to worship

ytebÄ

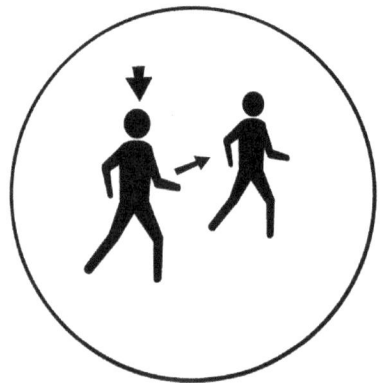

to chase

INTERACTION - VERB - ÄMEL

yé<u>kh</u>u

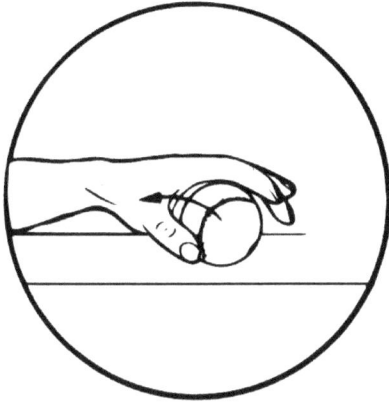

to get

y<u>sh</u>d

to hold

yqud

to lead

yĦel video

to play a video

yHot

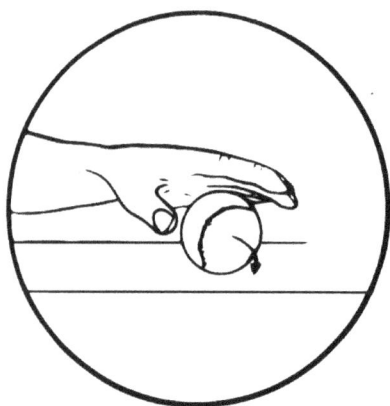

to put

ymes

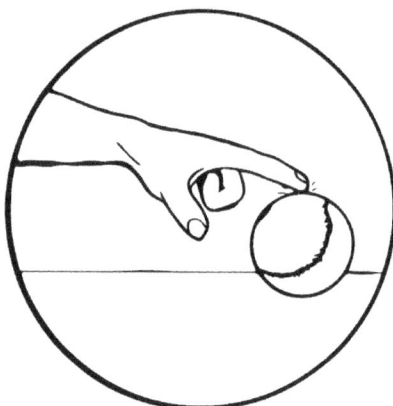

to touch

ytabteb

to pat

ymessaH

to rub

INTERACTION - VERB - ÄMEL

yarmi

to throw

yhez

to carry

ylem

to pick up

ydawar

to turn

ydhrab

to hit

ytayyaḤ

to drop

ysayib

to drop

yaqleb

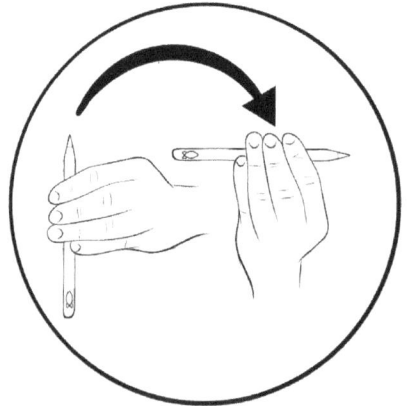

to turn

INTERACTION - VERB - ÄMEL

yHel

to open

yjbd

to pull

ydez

to push

ydawr

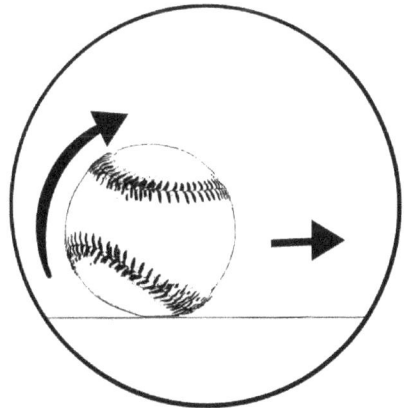

to roll

yarmi

to roll

yzarbt

to spin

yaℏfrr

to dig

yÄwwej

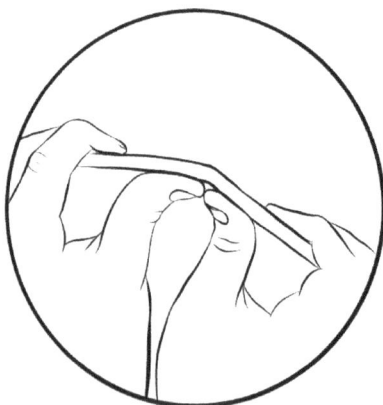

to bend

INTERACTION - VERB - ÄMEL

ythni

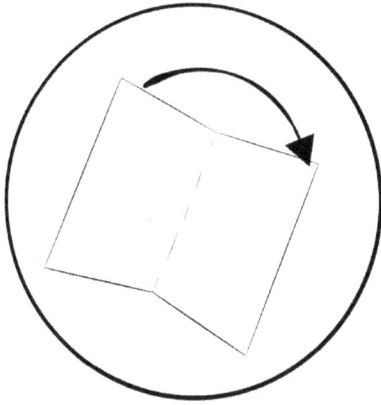

to fold

yÄsr

to squeeze

LIKID
LIQUID MOVEMENTS

ysob

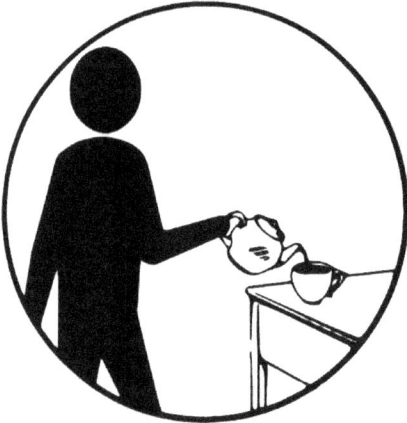

to pour

ybzzÄ

to spill

yqatr

to drip

ysiyl

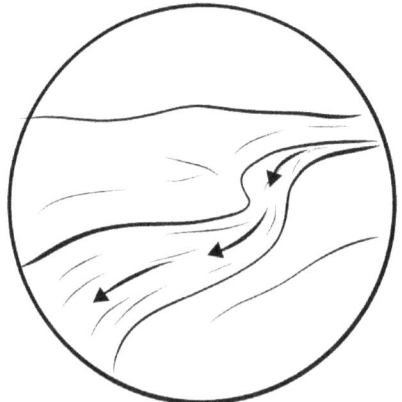

to flow

152

yqatr

to leak

shté tsob

to rain

yĦel mé

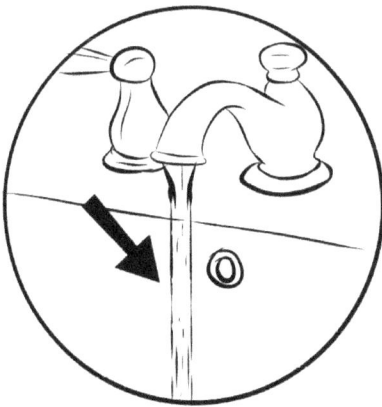

to run water

ytosh

to splash

YBEDL
TRANSFORMATION

yqos

to cut

yssawr

to draw

yfassa<u>kh</u>

to erase

ydawwr

to rotate

yziyd

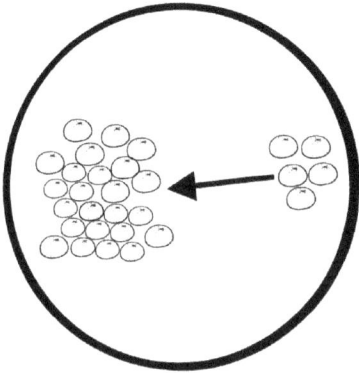

to add

yrakb

to assemble

ybni

to build

yqos

to chop

ysalaH

to fix

yezrÄ

to plant

y<u>kh</u>ayet

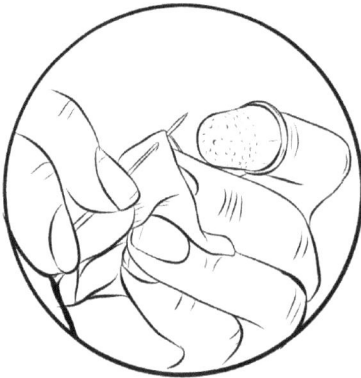

to sow

ykasr

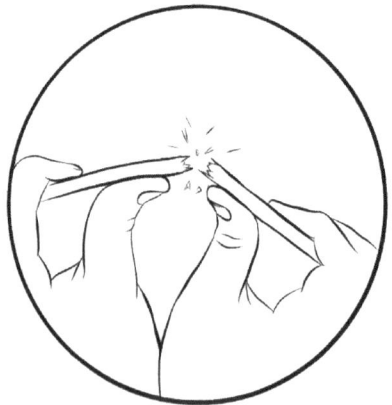

to break

TRANSFORMATION - VERB - YBEDL

yqatÄ

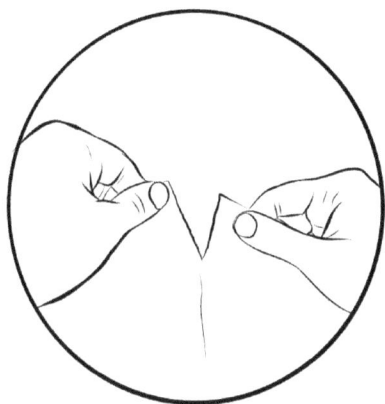

to rip

  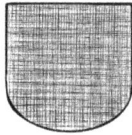 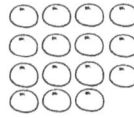 

 563 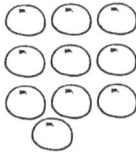 30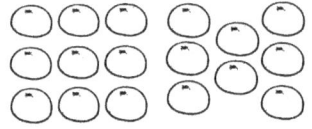

 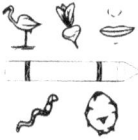  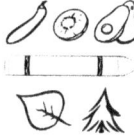 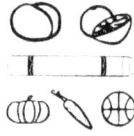 

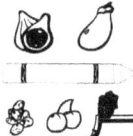 20 300 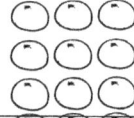 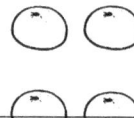 40

3

ŠIFET
DESCRIPTIONS

100

 50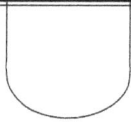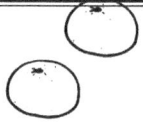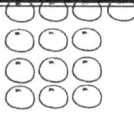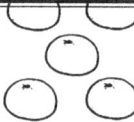

 85 200 90 60 80

500 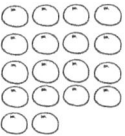 71 70 400 432

YMLEK
OWNERSHIP

m'téÄo | m'téĦa

his | hers

mtéÄi

my

mtéÄana

our

mteÄhom

their

mtéÄak

mtéÄakom

your

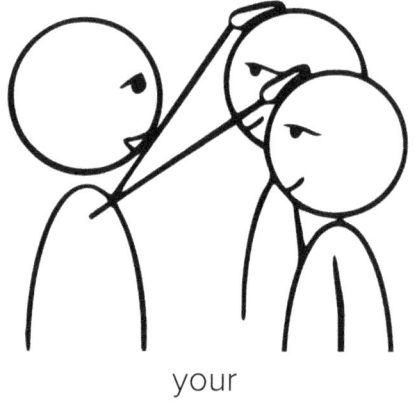

your

OWNERSHIP - DESCRIPTION - YMLEK

ELUWEN
COLORS

e<u>kh</u>el | kaĦla

black

azraq | zarqa

blue

boni | bonéa

brown

a<u>kh</u>dhar | <u>kh</u>a<u>dh</u>ra

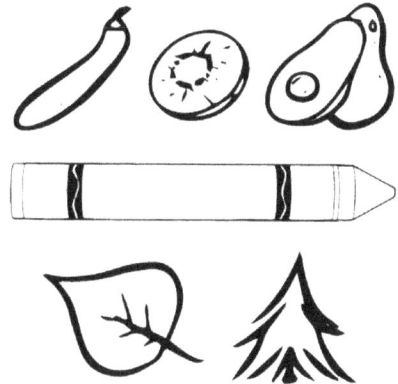

green

gri

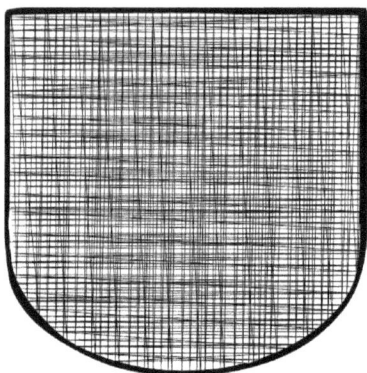

grey

bortuqali | bortuqalia

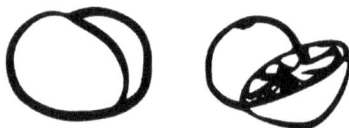

orange

ros

pink

mov

purple

a'Ḥmr | Ḥamra

red

abya<u>dh</u> | bi<u>dh</u>a

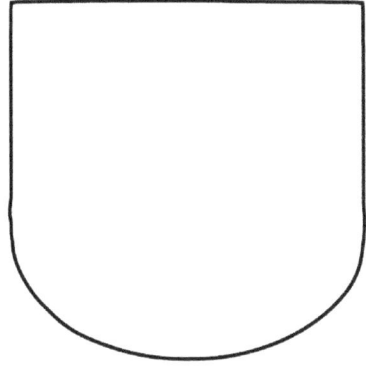

white

asfr | safra

yellow

ÄDED 1-20
NUMBERS 1-20

wéHed

thnin

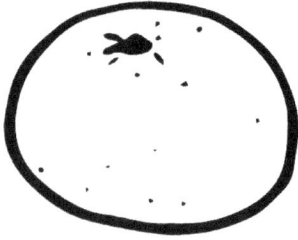

one

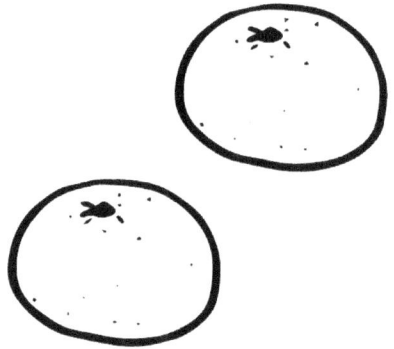

two

tlé'tha

arbÄ

three

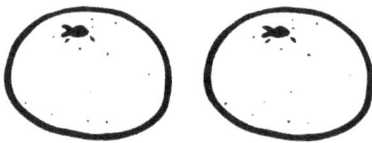

four

khamsa

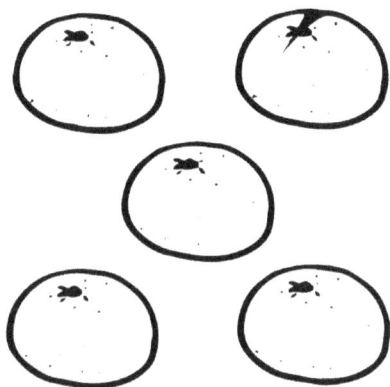

five

setta

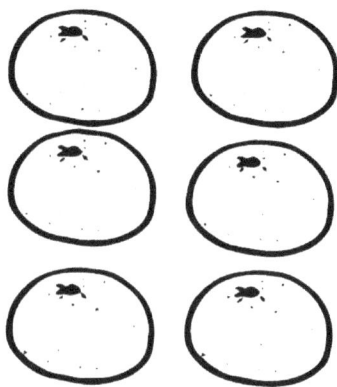

six

sabÄ

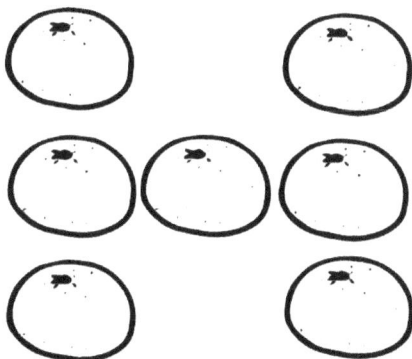

seven

thmenya

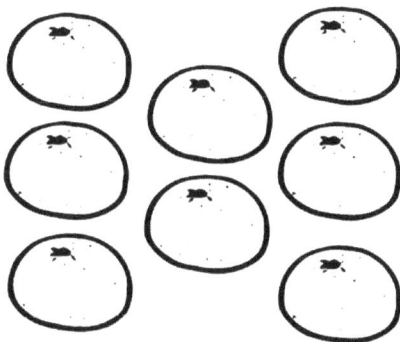

eight

ts'Ä

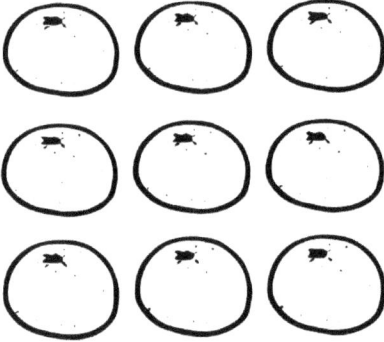

nine

Äsharah

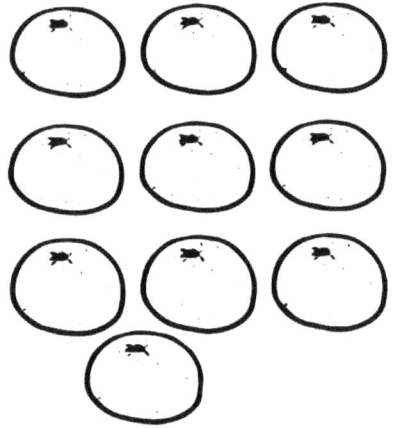

ten

Ħde'esh

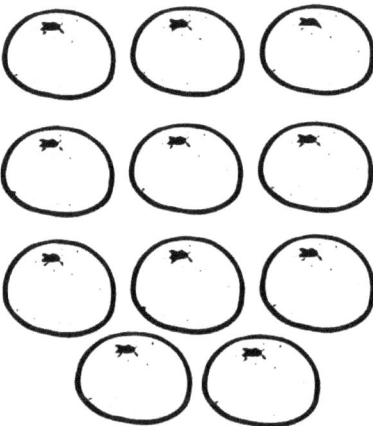

eleven

athnash

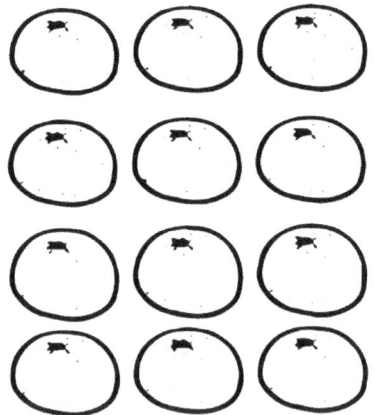

twelve

NUMBERS 1-20 - DESCRIPTION - ÄDED 1-20

thlotash

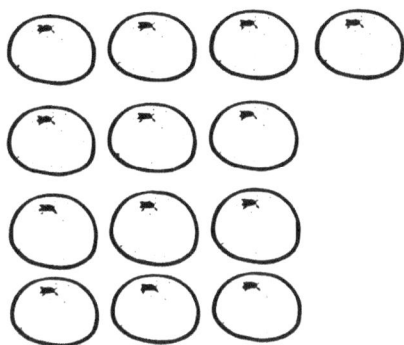

thirteen

arbÄtash

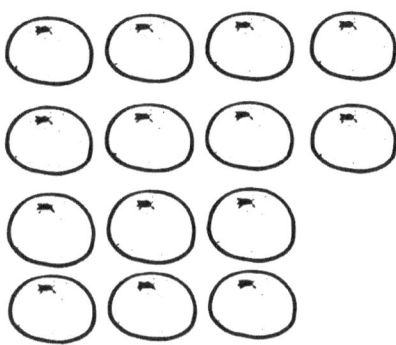

fourteen

khomastash

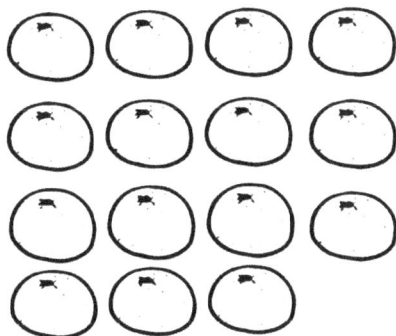

fifteen

sotash

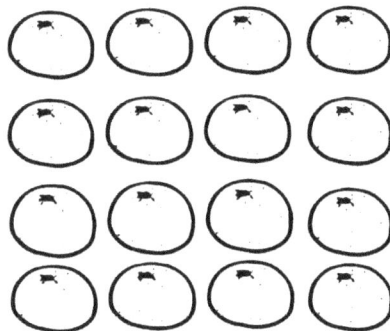

sixteen

sbÄta<u>sh</u>

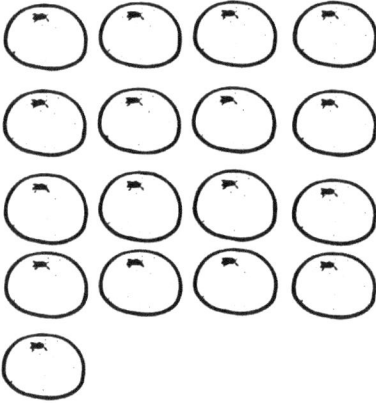

seventeen

<u>th</u>montas<u>h</u>

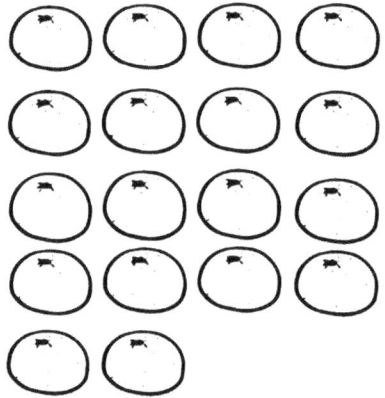

eighteen

tsÄta<u>sh</u>

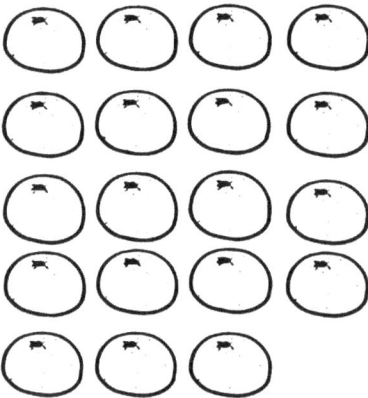

nineteen

Ä<u>sh</u>riin

20

twenty

ÄDED 20 +
NUMBERS (20+)

tléthin

30

thirty

arbÄ u tléthin

34

thirty four

arbÄ'in

40

forty

khamsin

50

fifty

settin

60

sixty

sabÄ'in

70

seventy

wehed u sabÄ'in

71

seventy one

thmenin

80

eighty

khamsa u thmenin

85

eighty five

tisÄ'in

90

ninety

mié'

100

one hundred

mitin

200

two hundred

tlétha mié'

300

three hundred

arbÄ mié'

400

four hundred

arbÄ mié' u ethnina u tléthin

432

four hundred thirty two

khamsa mié'

500

five hundred

khamsa mié' u tlétha u setin

setta mié'

563

600

five hundred sixty three

six hundred

sabÄ mié'

sabÄ mié' u arbÄ u setin

700

764

seven hundred

seven hundred sixty four

thmenya mié'

800

eight hundred

thmenya mié' u tsÄ u tsÄ'in

899

eight hundred ninety nine

tisÄ mié'

900

nine hundred

elf

1000

one thousand

elfin

2000

two thousand

elfin u <u>kh</u>amsa mié' u tlé<u>th</u>in

2530

two thousand five hundred thirty

tlé<u>th</u>a lef

3000

three thousand

arbÄ lef

4000

four thousand

khamsa lef

5000

five thousand

setta lef

6000

six thousand

sabÄ lef

7000

seven thousand

thmenya lef

8000

eight thousand

NUMBERS (20+) - DESCRIPTION - ÄDED 20 +

tisÄ lef

9000

nine thousand

Äsharah lef

10000

ten thousand

miét alf

100000

one hundred thousand

meliyun

1000000

one million

KEMMÉA
QUANTITY

shawaya

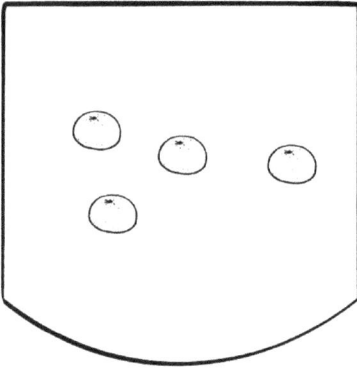

a few

shawaya mn

a little bit

ay waHda

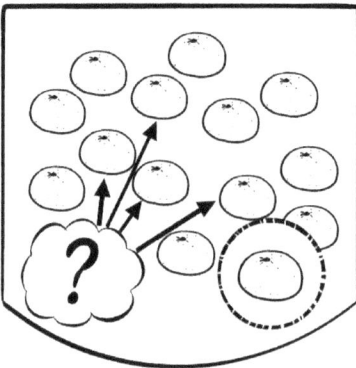

any one

kol waHda

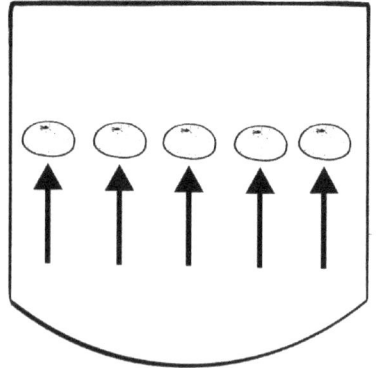

each one

kol

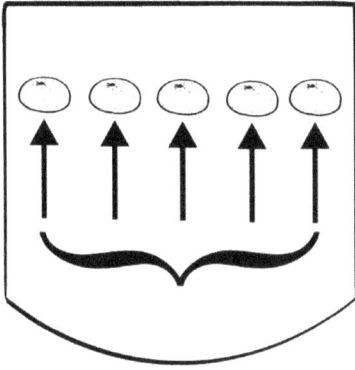

every one

aqal men

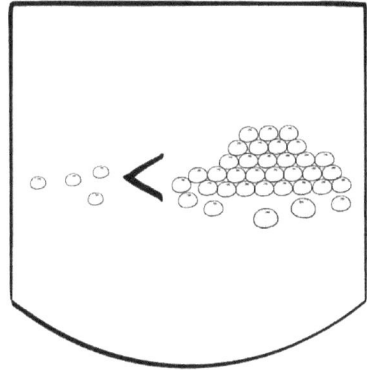

less than

ak<u>the</u> men

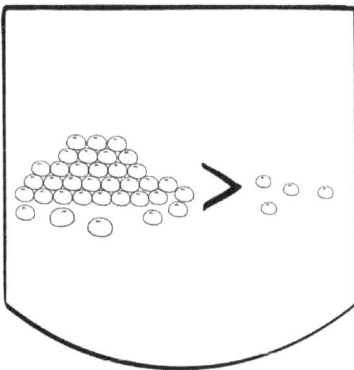

more than

muk<u>the</u>riet

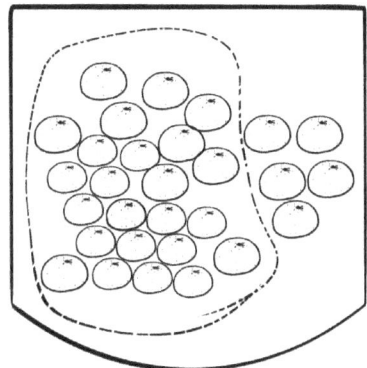

most of them

férgha

empty

mÄbi

full

m<u>sh</u> mÄbi

half-full

<u>sh</u>awaya mn

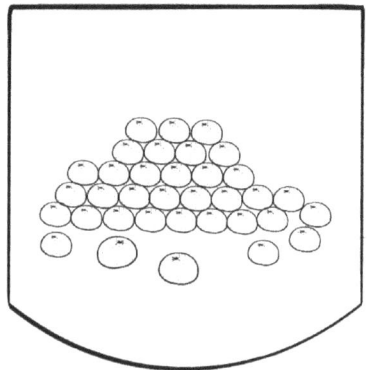

a bunch of

shawaya mn

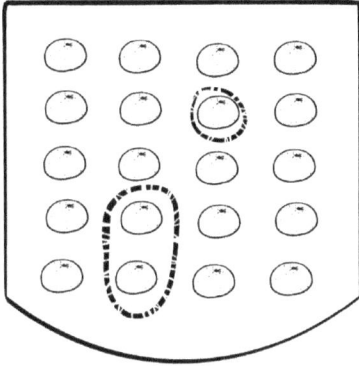

a couple of

barsha mnhom

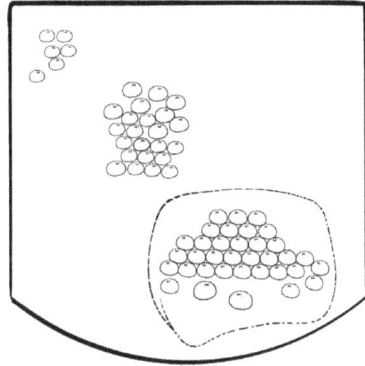

a lot of them

kolhom

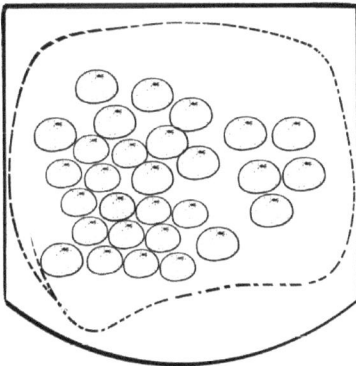

all of them

kol wéhed mnhom

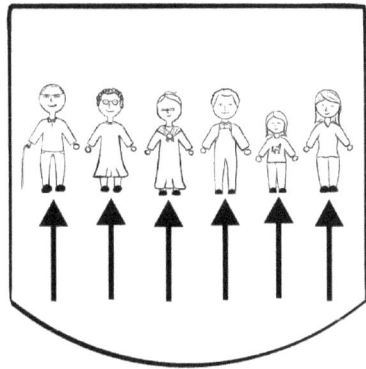

each of them

wéhed mnhom

one of them

shawaya mnhom

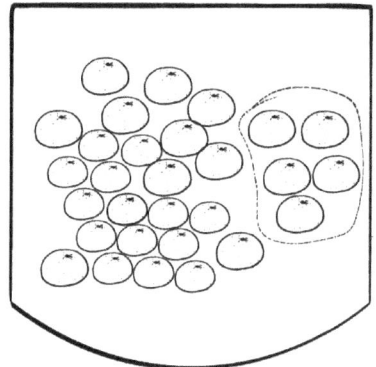

some of them

ĦattÄ Ħad

no one

shay'

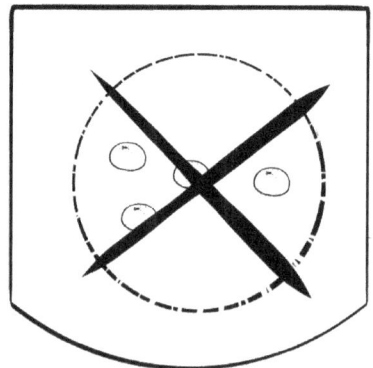

nothing

QUANTITY - DESCRIPTION - KEMMÉA

KOBR

SIZE

twil

tall

qsir

short

kbira

big

sghira

small

sghir

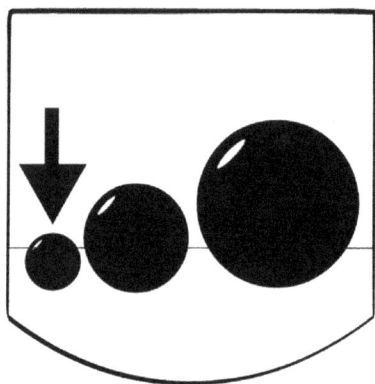

small

qasir

short

mtwasset

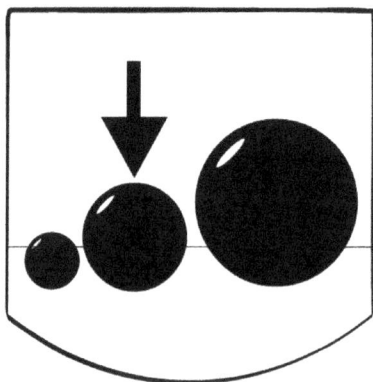

medium

kabir

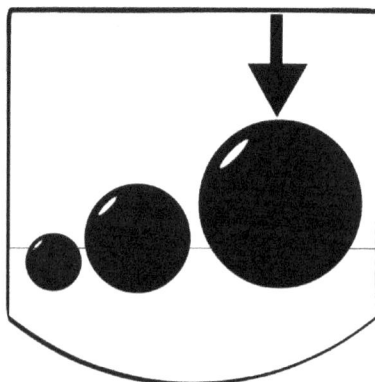

large

SIZE - DESCRIPTION - KOBR

qarib

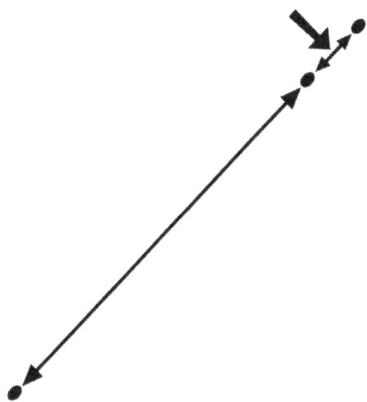

close

bÄ'id

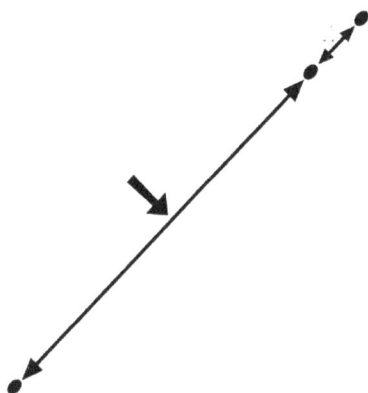

far

twil

long

atwel mn

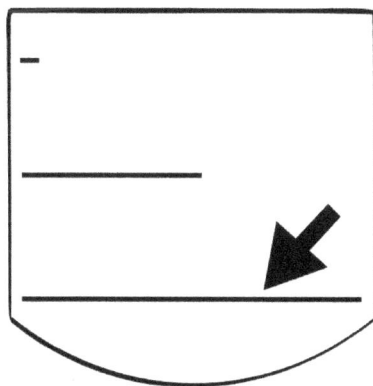

longer

ENWÉÄ DIREKSION
TYPES OF DIRECTION

Äl ysar

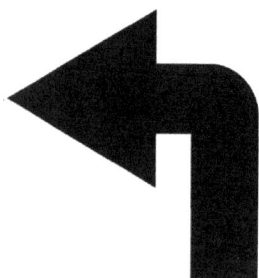

left turn

Äl ymin

right turn

touwl

straight

dur bilÄks

u-turn

mÄuj

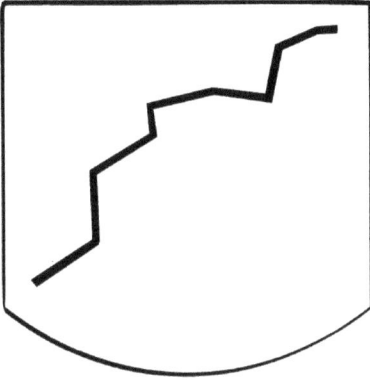

crooked

mqawes

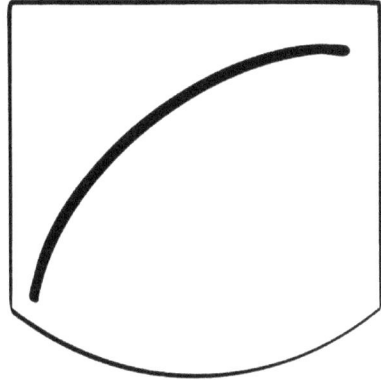

curved

mstwi

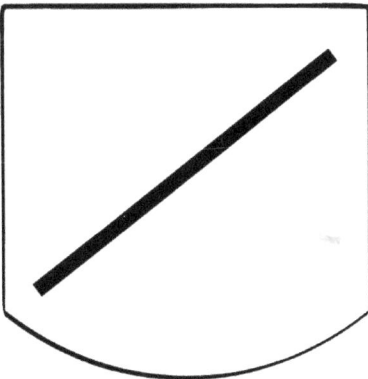

straight

WIN ? | FIIN ?
PLACEMENT

wora

behind

bjmb / baḤdha

beside

mé'bin

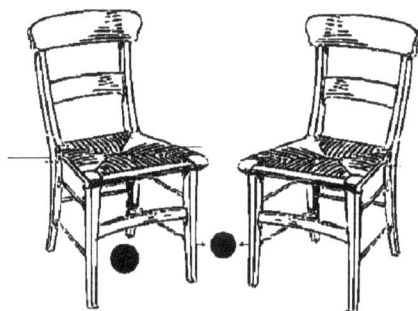

between

fi wst

in

wora

behind

fi

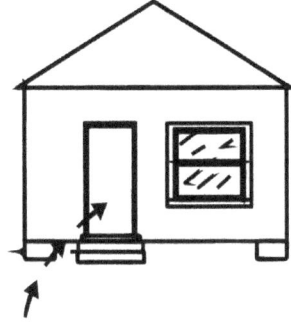

in

qodém

in front of

fuq

on

lbara

out

fuq

over

lbara

out

fuq

over

PLACEMENT - DESCRIPTION - WIN ? | FIIN ?

taHt

under

qodém

across

qÄa

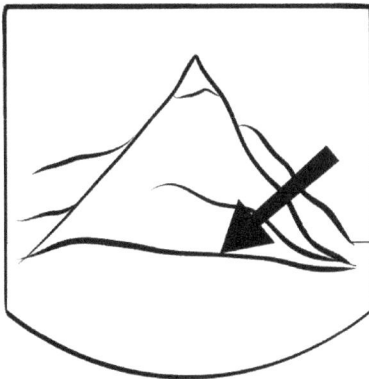

bottom

luta

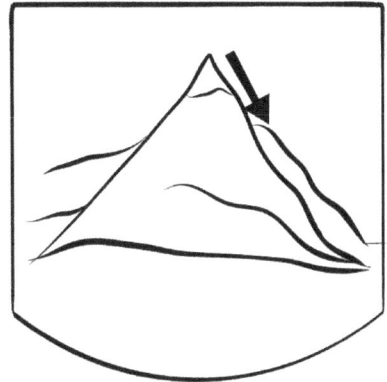

down

qodém

across

tHat

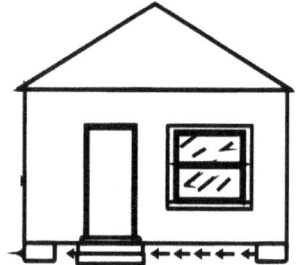

under

wst

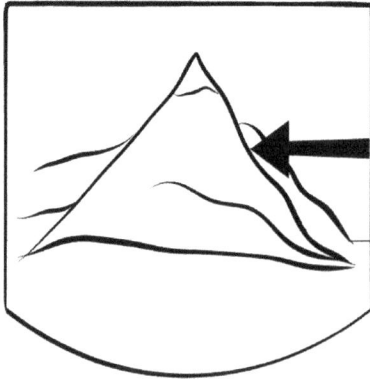

middle

tengura

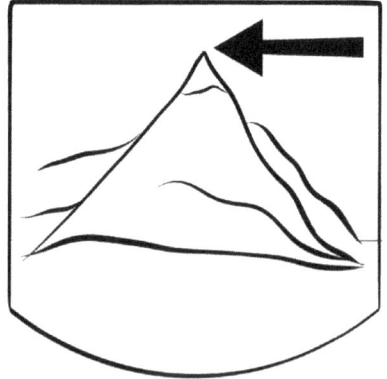

top

fuq

up

déyr

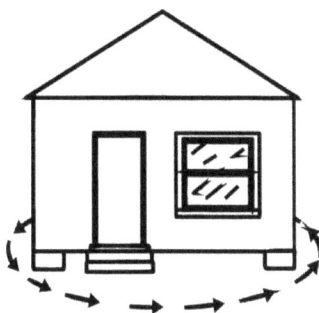

around

fi wst

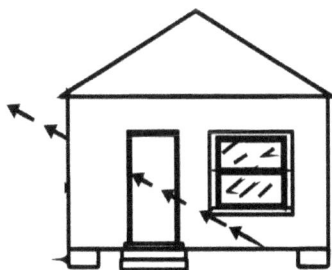

through

AHASSIS
FEELINGS

mtgha<u>sh</u>e<u>sh</u>

angry

féded

bored

berdén

cold

dé<u>kh</u>l ba<u>dh</u>u

confused

béred

cold

mbéyel

exhausted

farĦan

happy

s'<u>kh</u>oun

hot

jiÄn

hungry

s'<u>kh</u>oun

hot

maujuÄ

hurt

Ħazin

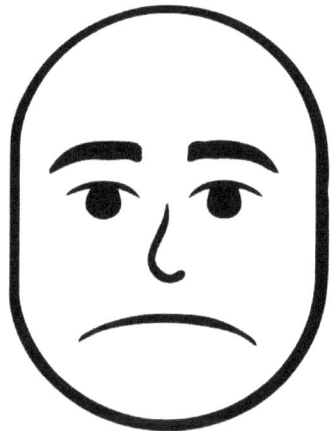

sad

FEELINGS - DESCRIPTION - AĦASSIS

behet

shocked

mridh

sick

mt'féja'

surprised

Äotshen

thirsty

t'éÄb

tired

mtqaleq

worried

yaghli

boiling

bered

cool

shéyaH

dry

mthelj

frozen

dćfii

warm

mebloul

wet

SHAKHSIA
CHARACTER DESCRIPTIONS

mehbul

crazy

mzawr

cunning

massakh

dirty

khayib

evil

farHan

jolly

behi

kind

ras mskr

stern

JENSIYYET
NATIONALITIES

Ämerekani

American

Ämerekia

American

Bengaladeshi

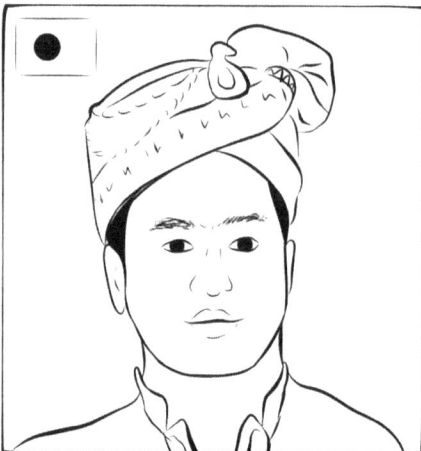
Bangladeshi

Bengaladeshia

Bangladeshi

Brazili

Brazilian

Brazilia

Brazilian

Englizi

British

Englizia

British

Kanadi

Canadian

Kanadia

Canadian

Sini

Chinese

Sinia

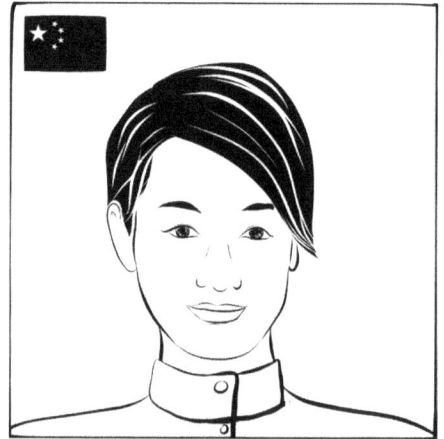

Chinese

NATIONALITIES - DESCRIPTION - JENSIYYET

Kongoli

Congolese

Kongolia

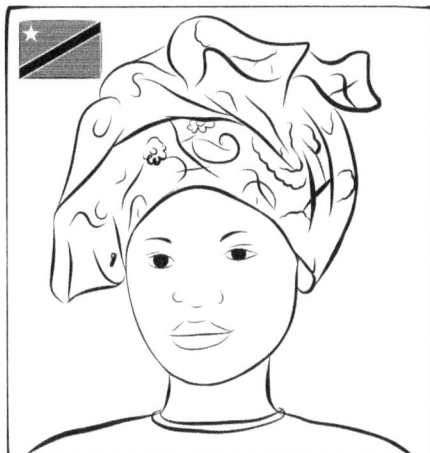

Congolese

Masri

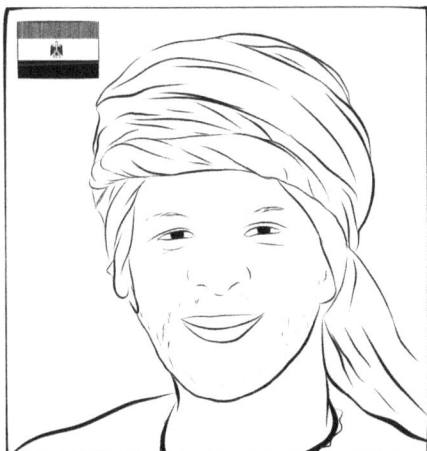

Egyptian

Masria

Egyptian

Ethiopi

Ethiopian

Ethiopia

Ethiopian

Fransawi

French

Fransawia

French

Älmani

German

Älmania

German

Ħindi

Indian

Ħindia

Indian

Endonisi

Indonesian

Endonisia

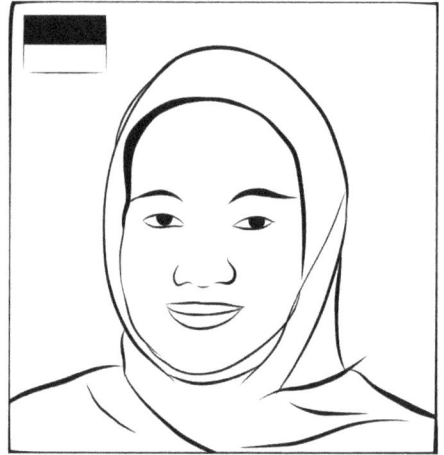

Indonesian

Irani

Iranian

Irania

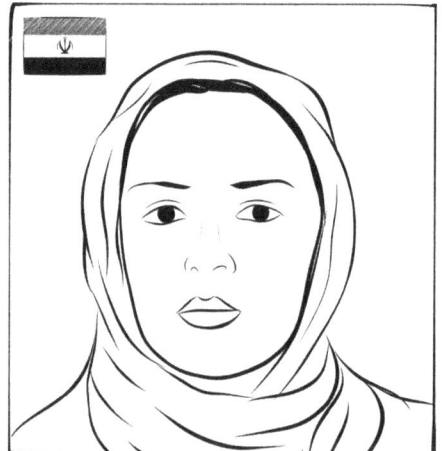

Iranian

NATIONALITIES - DESCRIPTION - JENSIYYET

Japoni

Japanese

Japonia

Japanese

Meksiki

Mexican

Meksikia

Mexican

Nijiri

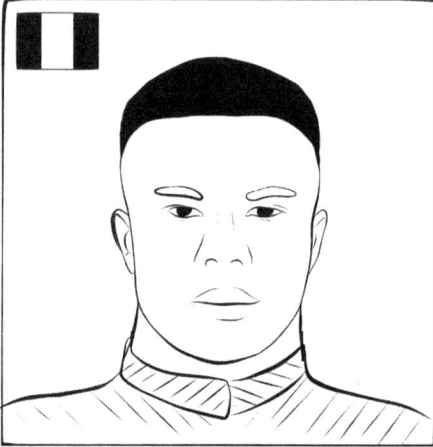

Nigerian

Nijiria

Nigerian

Pakisténi

Pakistani

Pakisténia

Pakistani

NATIONALITIES - DESCRIPTION - JENSIYYET

Filipini

Philippine

Filipinia

Philippine

Rusi

Russian

Rusia

Russian

Sou'udi

Saudi Arabian

Sou'udia

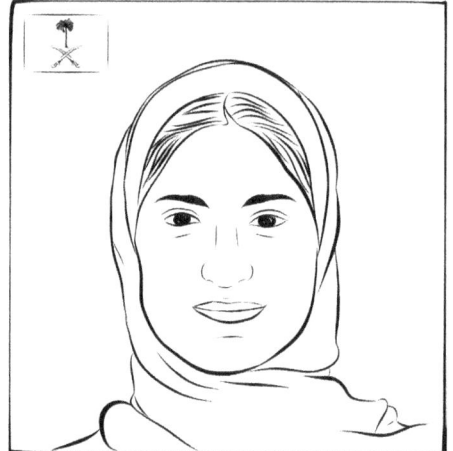

Saudi Arabian

Turki

Turkish

Turkia

Turkish

Viyetnami   Viyetnamia

Vietnamese

Vietnamese

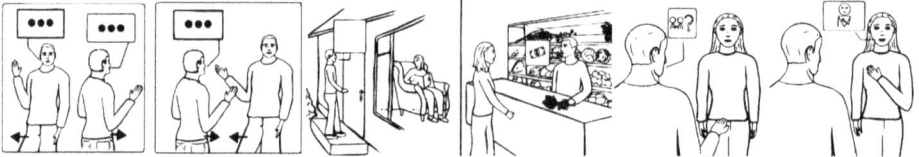

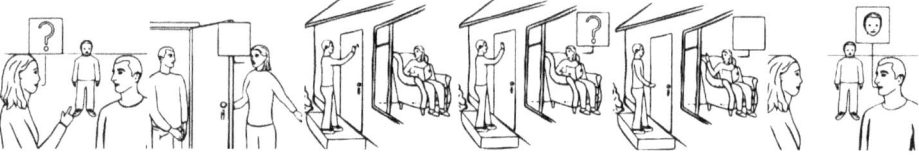

JUMEL
Phrases

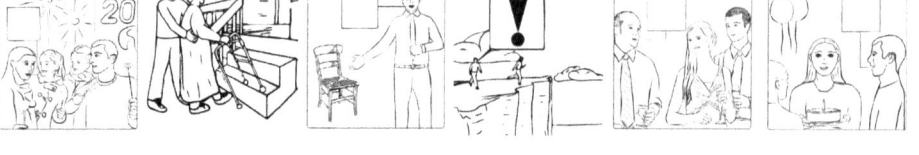

TESLIM
GREETINGS

Äsléma

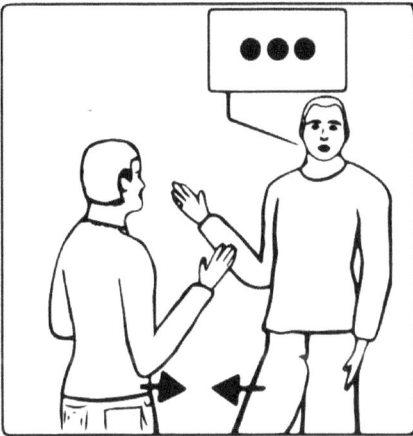

Hello.

Salem.

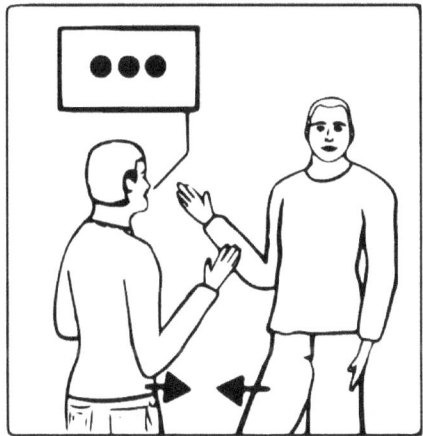

Hi.

Lebés ?

How are you ?

Lebés, inti lebés ?

I'm well. How are you?

Shnowa esmek?

What is your name ?

Esmi ...

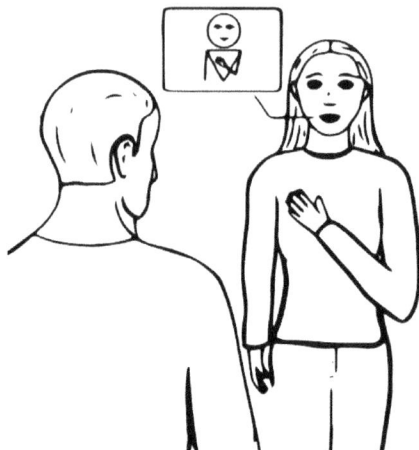

My name is ...

Shkunu howa ?

Who is he ?

Esmu ...

His name is ...

doq doq

knock knock

Shkun ?

Who is it ?

Ena howa !

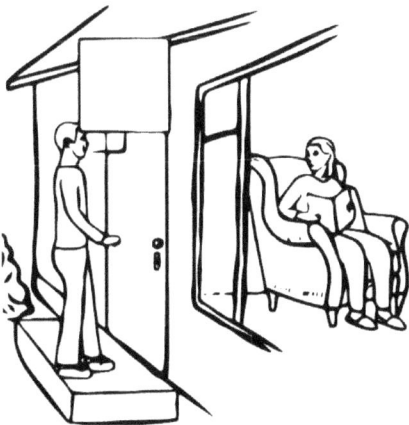

Its me!

Ħani jé ...

I'm coming...

MarHabé | tfadhel

Shukran .

Welcome. | Come on in!

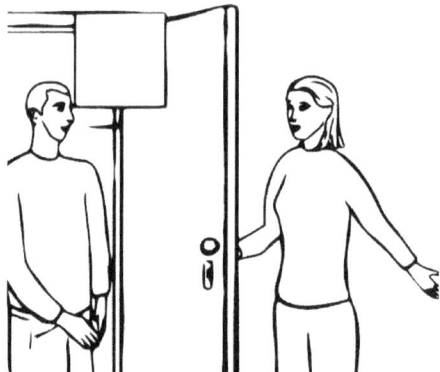

Thank you.

Bseléma

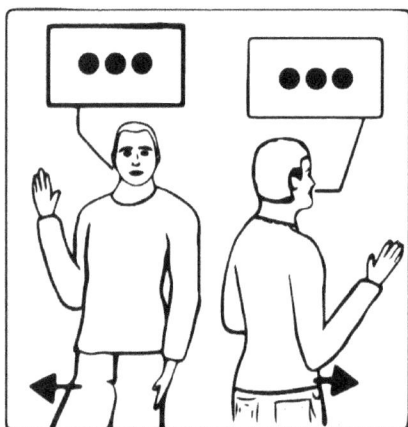

Goodbye.

GREETINGS - PHRASE - TESLIMET

JOMLET ÄDÉYA
COMMON PHRASES

klemferagh

Blah blah blah

samĦani, mfemteksh

I'm sorry, I don't understand ...

Shnowa he<u>dh</u>a ?

What is that

he<u>dh</u>a ...

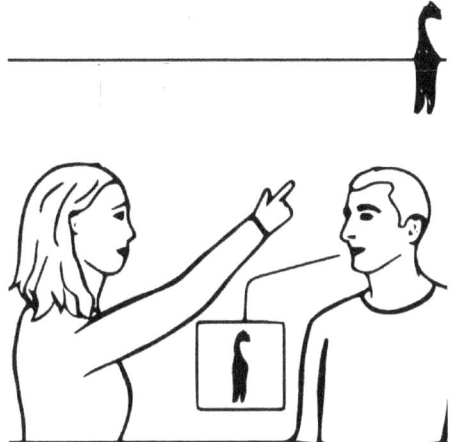

That is a ...

Shnowa he<u>dh</u>i ?

What is this ?

M'nÄre<u>sh</u>

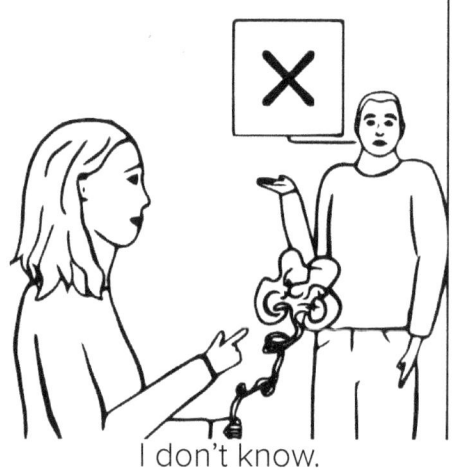

I don't know.

Shnowa he<u>dh</u>i ?

What is this ??

he<u>dh</u>i ...

This is a ....

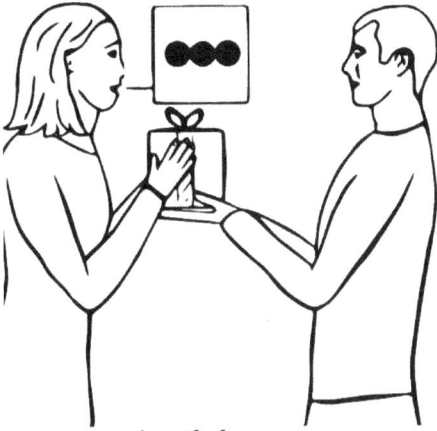
kado lik !
A gift for you

Äy<u>sh</u>ek
Thank you

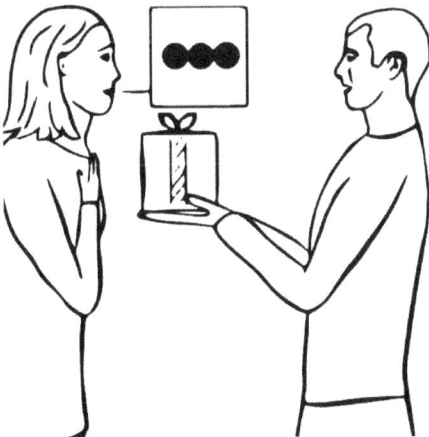
Mag<u>h</u>iyr mzéyya
You are welcome.

Ände'k ...
Do you have ... ?

É, Ändna …

Yes, we have … .

Win twalett ?

Where is the restroom?

Twalet ghadi .

The restroom is over there.

Qadesh hedhi?

How much is it?

hedhi ... dinar

It is ... dollars.

RaℏMek allah !

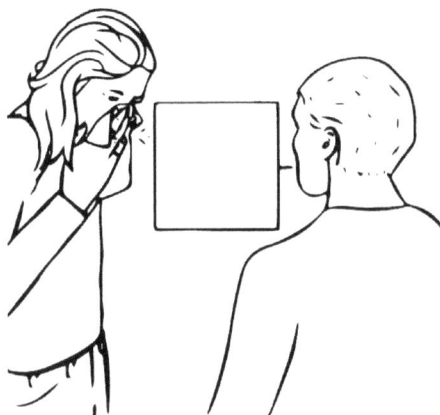

Bless you

Njem n'Äounek?

Can I help you?

É, yÄyshek .

Yes, please.

Rabi yfdhlek .

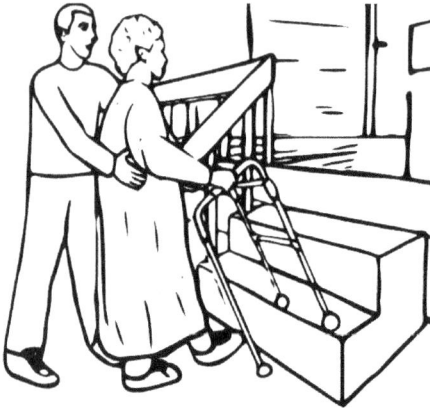

Thank you very much

Mséle<u>sh</u> t'Äouenni?

Can you help me?

É njem nÄounek.

Yes, I can help.

Shukran .

Thank you so much

Sotar!

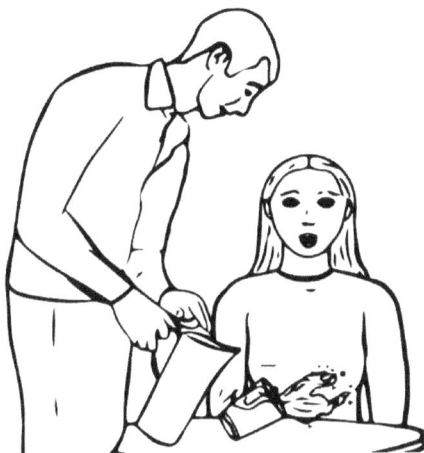

Oops!

SamaĦani..

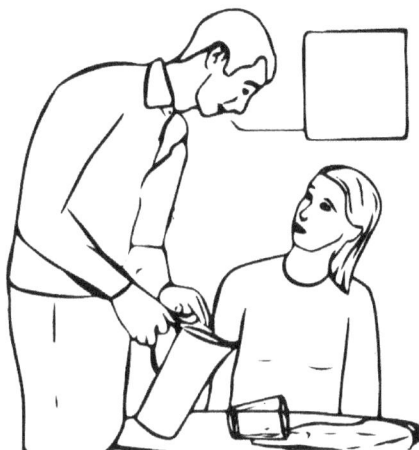

I'm sorry.

Lebés, msémĦek

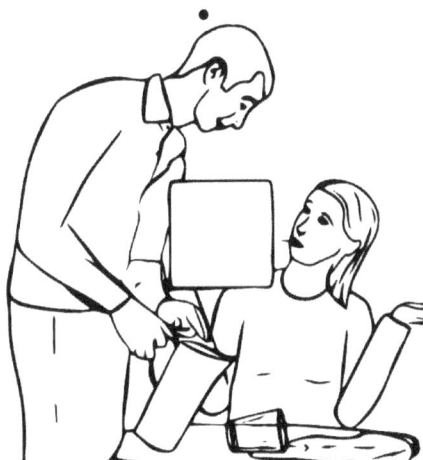

It's okay, I forgive you.

Rod bélek

Watch out!

T'Ħeb toqÄod ?

Please have a seat.

YaÄti nsiĦa

To give advice

Tnejm t'Äoudli ?

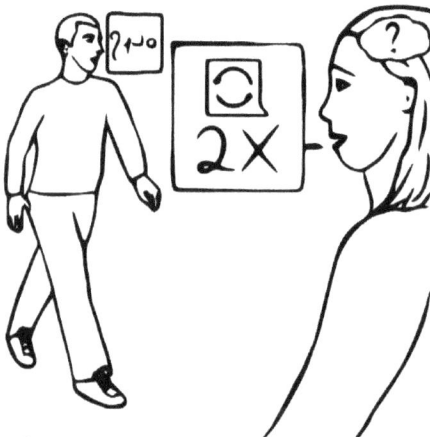

Can you repeat that for me?

Tnejm t'Äoudli bel aquéi?

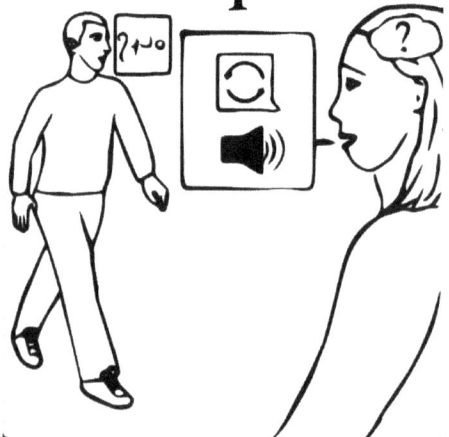

Can you say that louder?

Tnejm t'Äoudli beshawaya?

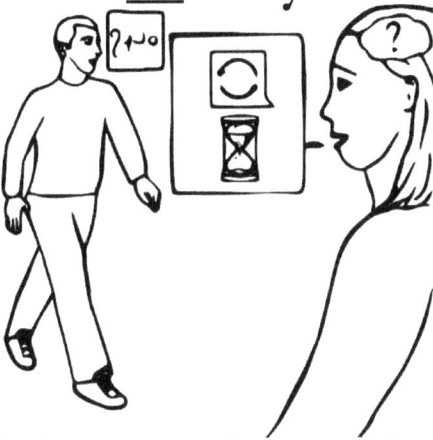

Can you say that slower?

Tnejm t'Äoudli bel Ḥarf bel Ḥarf

Can you spell that?

Mabrūk!

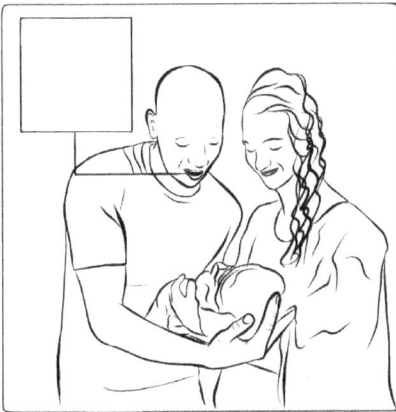

Congratulations!

Inshallah mabruk!

Best wishes to both of you!

Kull Äm wa inti b-<u>kh</u>ir !

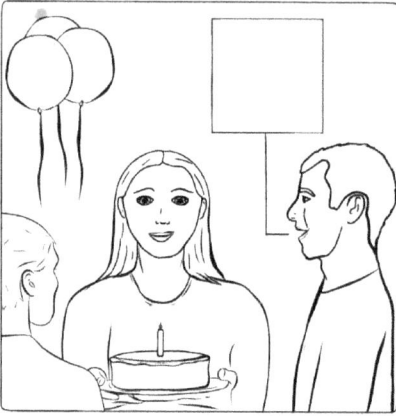

Happy birthday!

Ämek mabruk !

Happy new year!

El barka fik .

I'm sorry for your loss.

Index

blanket	89	canadian	204
blouse	33	candy	60
blow a nose	140	cap	34
blue	161	car	31
board	86	carrot	60
boat	30	carry	147
boiling	198	cat	18
bolt	82	cauliflower	60
book	85	ceiling	115
boot	33	chair	53
bored	194	chase	144
bottle	81	cheek	12
bottom	191	cherry	61
boy	4	chest	12
brazilian	203	chew	138
bread	59	chicken	21
break	156	children	5
british	203	chin	12
broccoli	59	chinese	204
brown	161	chop	137
brush	72	chop	155
build	155	church	45
bunch of	180	cilantro	61
bus	30	circle	27
bus station	44	claw	24
bush	93	climb	129
butcher	44	clock	87
buy	133	close	184
cabbage	59	clothes	41
cake	60	clothing store	45
call	134	cloud	93
camel	20	coat	34

worship	**144**
wrench	**84**
write	**133**
yawn	**142**
year	**105**
yellow	**163**
yesterday	**125**
you	**3**
you all	**3**
your	**160**
zucchini	**70**

www.ingramcontent.com/pod-product-compliance
Lightning Source LLC
Chambersburg PA
CBHW071213090426
42736CB00014B/2796